The Knitter's Guide to Combining Yarns

300 FOOLPROOF PAIRINGS

KATHLEEN GRECO
NICK GRECO

Bonus! 8 Projects

C&T PUBLISHING

© 2007 by Dimensional Illustrators, Inc.

Published by C&T Publishing, Inc., P.O. Box 1456, Lafayette, CA 94549; and Dimensional Illustrators, Inc., P.O. Box 543, Southampton, PA 18966, phone: 215-953-1415, email: jellyyarns@3dimillus.com, website: www.jellyyarns.com

Front cover: Spring Purse, Summer Sarong, and Fall Wrap
Back cover: Winter Sweater

Attention Teachers: C&T Publishing, Inc., encourages you to use this book as a text for teaching. Contact us at 800-284-1114 or www.ctpub.com for more information about the C&T Teachers Program.

We take great care to ensure that the information included in our books is accurate and presented in good faith, but no warranty is provided nor are results guaranteed. Having no control over the choices of materials or procedures used, neither the authors nor C&T Publishing, Inc., shall have any liability to any person or entity with respect to any loss or damage caused directly or indirectly by the information contained in this book. For your convenience, we post an up-to-date listing of corrections on our website (www.ctpub.com). If a correction is not already noted, please contact our customer service department at ctinfo@ctpub.com or at P.O. Box 1456, Lafayette, CA 94549.

Trademark (™) and registered trademark (®) names are used throughout this book. Rather than use the symbols with every occurrence of a trademark or registered trademark name, we are using the names only in the editorial fashion and to the benefit of the owner, with no intention of infringement.

Library of Congress Cataloging-in-Publication Data

Greco, Kathleen.
    The Knitter's guide to combining yarns : 300 foolproof pairings : bonus! 8 projects / Kathleen Greco and Nick Greco.
        p. cm.
    Includes index.
    ISBN-13: 978-1-57120-432-5 (paper trade : alk. paper)
    ISBN-10: 1-57120-432-6 (paper trade : alk. paper)
    1. Knitting--Patterns. 2. Yarn. I. Greco, Nick. II. Title.

TT820.G8243 2007
746.43'2041--dc22

                                                2007021725

Printed in China

10 9 8 7 6 5 4 3 2 1

Publisher *Amy Marson*

Editorial Director *Gailen Runge*

Acquisitions Editor *Jan Grigsby*

Creative Director / Creative Editor *Kathleen Greco Dimensional Illustrators, Inc.*

Executive Editor *Nick Greco Dimensional Illustrators, Inc.*

Book Design and Typography *Deborah Davis Deborah Davis Design*

Knitwear Designs *Kathleen Greco (pages 51, 66, 83, 98, 99)* and
Carrie A. Sullivan (pages 50, 51, 67, 82)

Fashion Photographer *Joe VanDeHatert Studio V*

Yarn Swatch Photography *Kathleen Greco Dimensional Illustrators, Inc.*

Sample Knitters *Carrie A. Sullivan and Judith Patkos*

Acknowledgments
Thank you to Amy Marson, Gailen Runge, and Jan Grigsby at C&T Publishing for their support.
A very special thanks to Deborah Davis for her graphic design.
Our appreciation to Joe VanDeHatert for his photographic genius,
and to our models for their style and poise.
Photos shot on location at the Nash Hotel, in South Beach, Florida.
Special thanks and appreciation to Carrie and Judith for their knitting expertise.
Our gratitude to Plymouth Yarns, Alchemy Yarns, Louisa Harding Yarns, Knitting to Know Ewe of
Penns Park, and Knit Together of Richboro, Pennsylvania, for their support and generosity.

Kathleen Greco and Nick Greco

INTRODUCTION

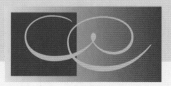

Tired of guessing which yarns look and work best when knit together? *The Knitter's Guide to Combining Yarns* takes the stress and guesswork out of combining yarns by providing beginning knitters a spectrum of color pairings for each season. You can wind two strands around your finger or use this guide to see the many combinations available when knitting different yarns together.

The *All About Yarns* chapter discusses essential fibers, including cotton, bamboo, silk, mohair, and wool, plus basic textures such as ribbon, bouclé, chenille, slubbed, and multi-strand. More than 25 colorful swatches reveal the most compatible yarn combinations. In the *Color Harmony* chapter you'll learn color wheel basics and how to coordinate colors, including monochromatic, analogous, complementary, black, white, and neutral color schemes. The *How to Substitute Yarns* chapter reviews the essential elements to consider when substituting yarns, including weight, gauge, fiber content, yarn characteristics, stitch definition, and yardage.

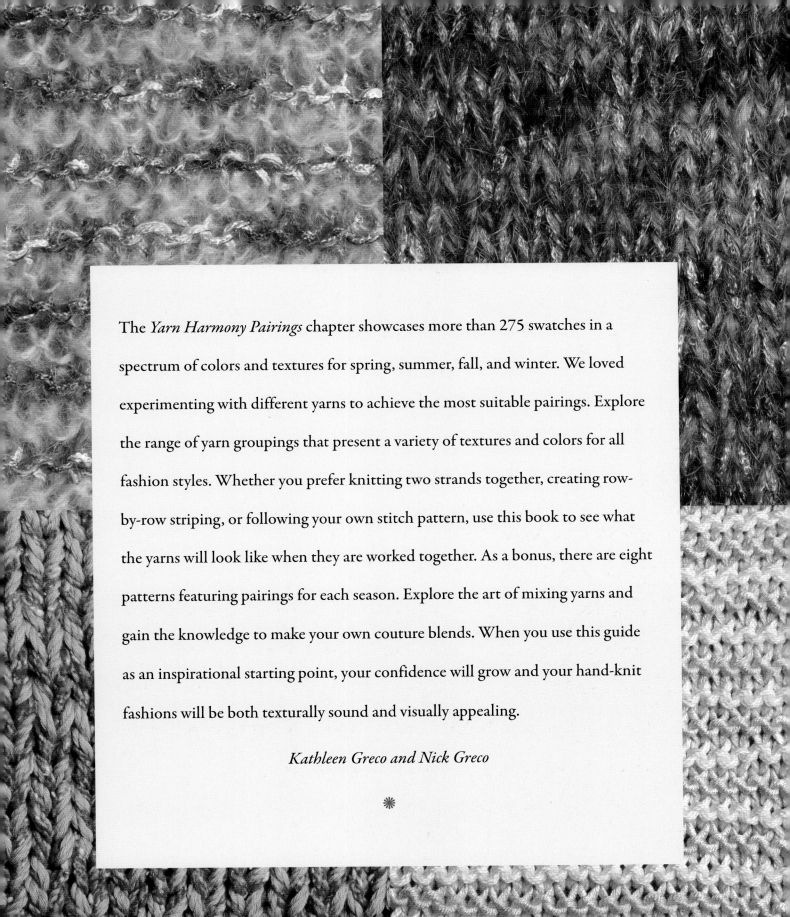

The *Yarn Harmony Pairings* chapter showcases more than 275 swatches in a spectrum of colors and textures for spring, summer, fall, and winter. We loved experimenting with different yarns to achieve the most suitable pairings. Explore the range of yarn groupings that present a variety of textures and colors for all fashion styles. Whether you prefer knitting two strands together, creating row-by-row striping, or following your own stitch pattern, use this book to see what the yarns will look like when they are worked together. As a bonus, there are eight patterns featuring pairings for each season. Explore the art of mixing yarns and gain the knowledge to make your own couture blends. When you use this guide as an inspirational starting point, your confidence will grow and your hand-knit fashions will be both texturally sound and visually appealing.

Kathleen Greco and Nick Greco

✳

1
ALL ABOUT YARNS

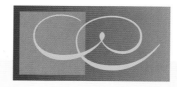

Discover the essential characteristics of all your favorite yarns. Each page in this chapter presents a different fiber or texture and discusses the principal qualities of ten of the most popular knitting yarns. Fashionable fibers include cotton, bamboo, silk, mohair, and wool, while the best yarns for texture include ribbon, bouclé, chenille, slubbed, and multi-strand yarns. Seasonal preferences and project ideas are highlighted. Details expose troubleshooting areas to anticipate when knitting. This section also includes helpful comments for working with that particular yarn. Learn the common variations of the fibers and the textural features of these trendsetter yarns. Colorful sample swatches show the most compatible yarns to knit together. Meet the yarns up close and personal for the first time if you're new to knitting, or treat yourself to a quick refresher if you've been knitting for years but are looking for new ideas. Explore the possibilities!

COTTON YARNS

CHARACTERISTICS : *classic favorite, lightweight, soft fiber, comfortable, and affordable*

COMMON VARIATIONS : *100% cotton, mercerized-cotton, cotton-bouclé, and cotton-ribbon blend yarns*

SEASONAL PREFERENCES : *spring, summer, fall*

PROJECT IDEAS : *tops, lightweight sweaters, cardigans, and small purses*

AVERAGE WEIGHT RANGE : *fine to bulky*

TROUBLESHOOTING : *non-stretch, snagging, shows stitch definition and mistakes easily*

COMPATIBLE PAIRING YARNS : *bamboo, ribbon, bouclé, or multi-strand yarns*

COMMENTS : *Excellent drape. Pairs well when it is combined with a textural yarn. Use as a second yarn to bulk up delicate yarns of a similar weight.*

Variegated Ribbon + Cotton Yarns

Wool Blend + Cotton Bouclé Blend Yarns

Bamboo + Cotton Twist Yarns

BAMBOO YARNS

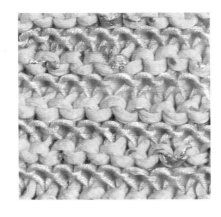

CHARACTERISTICS : *ultra soft fiber, naturally antibacterial, and ultraviolet protective qualities*

COMMON VARIATIONS : *100% bamboo, bamboo-wool, and bamboo-cotton blend yarns*

SEASONAL PREFERENCES : *spring, summer*

PROJECT IDEAS : *delicate tops, light wraps, sweaters, and baby knits*

AVERAGE WEIGHT RANGE : *fine to medium*

TROUBLESHOOTING : *splitting, snagging, shows stitch definition and mistakes easily*

COMPATIBLE PAIRING YARNS : *cotton, ribbon, or wool*

COMMENTS : *Excellent drape. Use to soften non-stretch yarns like cotton. Knitting slowly with blunt-end needles will help prevent the fine, multi-ply strands from splitting.*

Variegated Bamboo + Cotton Yarns

Variegated Bamboo + Ribbon Yarns

Multi-strand + Bamboo Yarns

SILK YARNS

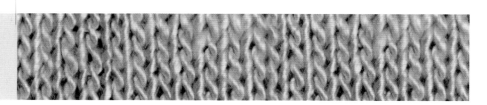

CHARACTERISTICS : *luxurious natural fiber, soft texture, lustrous shine, and extraordinary hand-dyed colors*

COMMON VARIATIONS : *100% silk, silk-linen, silk-wool, and silk-mohair blend yarns*

SEASONAL PREFERENCES : *spring, fall, winter*

PROJECT IDEAS : *scarves, fashion tops, sweaters, scarves, and wraps*

AVERAGE WEIGHT RANGE : *super fine to medium*

TROUBLESHOOTING : *splitting, snagging, shows stitch definition and mistakes easily*

COMPATIBLE PAIRING YARNS : *wool, mohair, alpaca, cotton, linen, or cashmere*

COMMENTS : *Excellent drape. Single-ply silk yarn has a tendency to snag on the needle. To prevent snagging, knit silk together with a second yarn.*

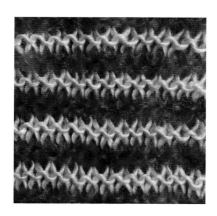

Silk Blend + Cotton Yarns

Silk Blend + Variegated Mohair Yarns

Wool Blend + Silk Blend Yarns

MOHAIR YARNS

CHARACTERISTICS : *natural fiber from the Angora goat, lightweight yet warm, and stronger than wool*

COMMON VARIATIONS : *100% mohair, brushed mohair, wool-mohair, and silk-mohair blend yarns*

SEASONAL PREFERENCES : *fall, winter*

PROJECT IDEAS : *tops, wraps, shawls, sweaters, coats, and scarves*

AVERAGE WEIGHT RANGE : *super fine to medium*

TROUBLESHOOTING : *snagging, when substituting fuzzy mohair for another yarn, test for stitch definition*

COMPATIBLE PAIRING YARNS : *wool, silk, or bouclé*

COMMENTS : *Mohair yarn is resistant to pilling and holds up well when dyed. Pairs well when a solid is combined with a variegated yarn.*

Variegated Mohair + Cotton Blend Yarns

Variegated Mohair Ribbon + Wool Yarns

Mohair + Bouclé Wool Yarns

WOOL YARNS

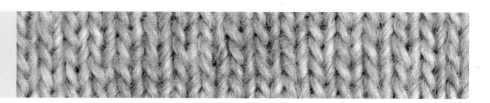

CHARACTERISTICS : *natural, super-soft fiber, derived principally from the fleece of sheep*

COMMON VARIATIONS : *100% wool, wool-mohair, wool-silk, wool-bouclé, and wool-slubbed blend yarns*

SEASONAL PREFERENCES : *fall, winter*

PROJECT IDEAS : *pullovers, sweaters, hats, purses, gloves, blankets, coats, socks, and scarves*

AVERAGE WEIGHT RANGE : *super fine to super bulky*

TROUBLESHOOTING : *wool shrinks when washed in hot water, and can be an allergenic*

COMPATIBLE PAIRING YARNS : *mohair, cashmere, or silk*

COMMENTS : *A traditional favorite, wool is perfect for felting. Wool is great for beginning knitters because it is highly forgiving and easy to work.*

Multi-strand Cotton Blend + Wool Yarns

Wool + Variegated Wool Slub Yarns

Multi-strand Wool Blend + Mohair Yarns

RIBBON YARNS

CHARACTERISTICS : *flat band yarn, with a soft, springy texture*

COMMON VARIATIONS : *synthetic, bamboo ribbon, cotton ribbon, silk ribbon, and mohair ribbon textural yarns*

SEASONAL PREFERENCES : *spring, summer, fall*

PROJECT IDEAS : *tops, light sweaters, scarves, shawls, and wraps*

AVERAGE WEIGHT RANGE : *fine to medium*

TROUBLESHOOTING : *wide ribbon splits easily, and wrinkles*

COMPATIBLE PAIRING YARNS : *bamboo, cotton, silk, or wool blends*

COMMENTS : *Flat or tape yarns are typically created from nylon, rayon, or polyester. The latest ribbon yarns are produced from natural fibers including cotton, linen, silk, mohair, and even wool.*

Ribbon + Cotton Yarns

Mohair Ribbon + Mohair Ribbon Yarns

Variegated Ribbon + Variegated Ribbon Yarns

BOUCLÉ YARNS

CHARACTERISTICS : *from the French word bouclér, "to curl", knotty textural yarn with loops*

COMMON VARIATIONS : *wool bouclé, mohair bouclé, and cotton bouclé textural yarns*

SEASONAL PREFERENCES : *spring, summer, fall, winter*

PROJECT IDEAS : *tops, bulky sweaters, cardigans, scarves, and blankets*

AVERAGE WEIGHT RANGE : *fine to bulky*

TROUBLESHOOTING : *stitch mistakes are hard to see and difficult to frog (undo)*

COMPATIBLE PAIRING YARNS : *wool, mohair, silk, or cotton*

COMMENTS : *For a colorful textural effect, knit a solid color yarn with a variegated bouclé yarn. To prevent unraveling, tie a secure knot at the end of the yarn strands.*

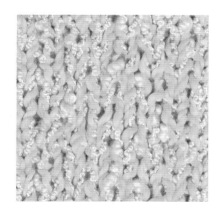

Cotton + Cotton Blend Bouclé Yarns

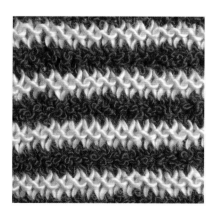

Silk Blend + Bouclé Wool Blend Yarns

Mohair + Bouclé Wool Blend Yarns

CHENILLE YARNS

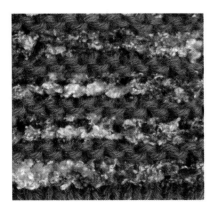

CHARACTERISTICS : *ultra soft textural yarn, created from short lengths of fabric plies*

COMMON VARIATIONS : *cotton chenille, wool chenille, and silk chenille textural yarns*

SEASONAL PREFERENCES : *fall, winter*

PROJECT IDEAS : *baby knits, blankets, pullovers, cardigans, and scarves*

AVERAGE WEIGHT RANGE : *fine to bulky*

TROUBLESHOOTING : *non-stretch, sheds, not reusable if you frog (undo) your stitches*

COMPATIBLE PAIRING YARNS : *cotton, wool, or bouclé*

COMMENTS : *Knit chenille together with another yarn to ease stretching and control worming. Keep stitches and tension tight.*

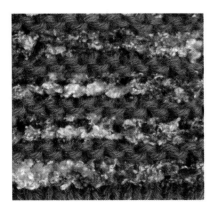

Wool Blend + Chenille Yarns

Chenille + Cotton Blend Yarns

Variegated Chenille + Wool Yarns

SLUBBED YARNS

CHARACTERISTICS : *thin and thick clumps of fiber on a central strand producing a bumpy texture*

COMMON VARIATIONS : *wool slubbed, cotton slubbed, and silk slubbed textural yarns*

SEASONAL PREFERENCES : *spring, summer, fall, winter*

PROJECT IDEAS : *tops, sweaters, purses, hats, coats, and scarves*

AVERAGE WEIGHT RANGE : *light to bulky*

TROUBLESHOOTING : *caution when knitting buttonholes*

COMPATIBLE PAIRING YARNS : *wool, cotton, or silk*

COMMENTS : *Tone down a variegated slubbed yarn by pairing it with a solid of a similar weight. Add texture to a single plain fiber by pairing it with a slubbed yarn.*

Wool Slub + Variegated Wool Slub Yarns

Cotton Blend Slub + Cotton Yarns

Cotton + Cotton Blend Slub Yarns

MULTI-STRAND YARNS

CHARACTERISTICS : *comprised of two or more different compatible fibers for a textual yarn*

COMMON VARIATIONS : *cotton, wool, metallic, mohair, silk, natural and synthetic multi-strand textural yarns*

SEASONAL PREFERENCES : *spring, summer, fall, winter*

PROJECT IDEAS : *tops, sweaters, cardigans, purses, scarves, and wraps*

AVERAGE WEIGHT RANGE : *super fine to super bulky*

TROUBLESHOOTING : *often splits easily*

COMPATIBLE PAIRING YARNS : *cotton, wool, mohair, silk, or bamboo*

COMMENTS : *Multi-strand yarns differ from fiber blends in that two or more yarns are twisted together instead of spun together to form a single strand.*

Multi-strand Cotton Blend + Cotton Blend Yarns

Multi-strand Cotton Blend + Wool Yarns

Multi-strand Cotton + Cotton Yarns

2
COLOR HARMONY

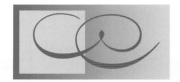

The first thing that impresses us when we visit a yarn shop is the brilliant array of colorful yarns. We identify ourselves by choosing and wearing our favorite colors. Color defines our personality and our individuality. The purpose of this chapter is to help you understand and learn color relationships so you can use balanced yarn combinations in your knitting projects. ✳ In this chapter, we discuss color basics and the six fundamental color relationships: monochromatic, analogous, complementary, white plus a color, black plus a color, and neutral plus a color. The yarn pairings in Chapter 4 show examples using these six fundamental relationships, knit with yarns in six basic primary and secondary colors. ✳ The same color principles apply when combining yarns as when mixing paints. However, when you are knitting with two or more color strands, their proximity changes the appearance of the yarn. Because color is a personal choice there is no right or wrong way to combine colors, but using color harmony will allow you to create balanced color combinations. The power of color is at your fingertips.

COLOR BASICS

The basics of color theory will help you understand how colors are created and their relationships to each other. The graphic below shows the color positions on a standard color wheel. Notice that the three primary colors—yellow, red, and blue—are equidistant from each other. These three basic colors are special because they cannot be created from other colors.

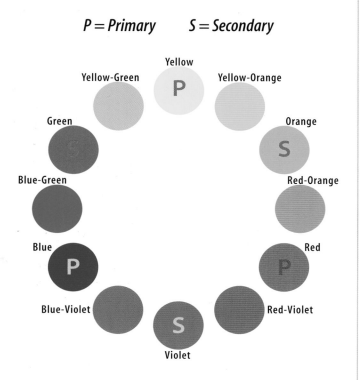

P = Primary   S = Secondary

Halfway between the three primary colors lie the three secondary colors: orange, violet, and green. In between the primary and secondary colors are the six tertiary colors: yellow-orange, red-orange, red-violet, blue-violet, blue-green, and yellow-green. There are many possible color combinations. Mixing white with a color changes the tint. Mixing black with a color changes the shade. Mix two colors together and you change the color. The color wheel is a reliable reference tool for creating perfectly balanced yarn combinations.

COLOR MIXING

Use the three primary colors—yellow, red, and blue—to create the secondary colors. See the graphic below. Create green by mixing yellow and blue. Create violet by mixing blue and red. Make orange by mixing red and yellow. By using different saturations (changing the brightness or intensity) of primary colors, many secondary color variations are possible.

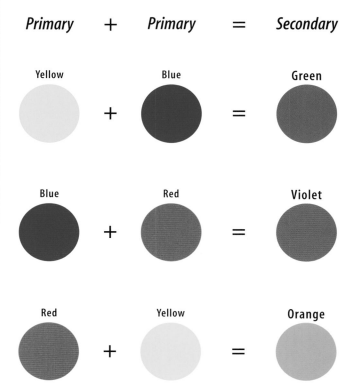

Primary   +   Primary   =   Secondary

Mix the primary and secondary colors to create the tertiary colors. Refer to the color wheel. Yellow-orange (apricot) is made by mixing yellow and orange. Red-orange (tomato) is made by mixing red and orange. Red-violet (plum) is made by mixing red and violet. Blue-violet (periwinkle) is made by mixing blue and violet. Blue-green (teal) is made by mixing blue and green. Yellow-green (chartreuse) is made by mixing yellow and green. This standard color system is the basis for mixing all color combinations.

YARN MIXING

When two or more color strands are knit together, the proximity of the two colors alters the appearance of the yarns—for example, they might seem brighter, darker, warmer, cooler, or more balanced. Unlike when you mix a liquid medium, such as paint, when you knit two strands together you do not create a third color. The juxtaposition of the yarns knit together create an overall color texture.

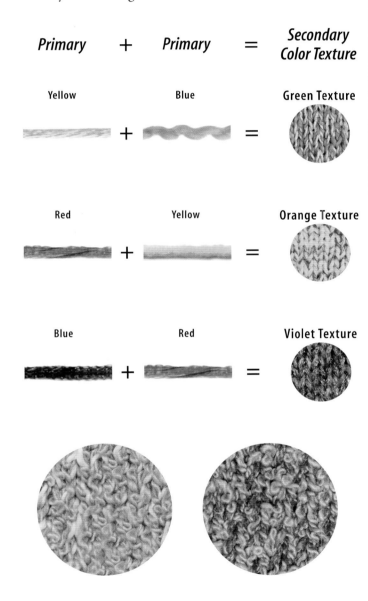

Primary	**+**	*Primary*	**=**	*Secondary Color Texture*
Yellow	+	Blue	=	**Green Texture**
Red	+	Yellow	=	**Orange Texture**
Blue	+	Red	=	**Violet Texture**

Here are two swatches using the SAME blue-violet yarn knit with different color yarns. In the left circle, blue-violet yarn is knit with bright yellow yarn. In the right circle blue-violet yarn is knit with dark violet yarn. The blue-violet yarn appears brighter when knit with a color closest on the color wheel. The blue-violet yarn appears paler when knit with a brighter color located on the opposite side of the color wheel.

MONOCHROMATIC YARNS

Monochromatic colors (*mono* meaning *"one"*) utilize only one color family. Create simple, balanced two-toned color effects by combining yarns of the same color in different shades. Examples of monochromatic color combinations include yellow + chiffon, orange + apricot, red + pink, violet + plum, blue + light blue, and green + olive.

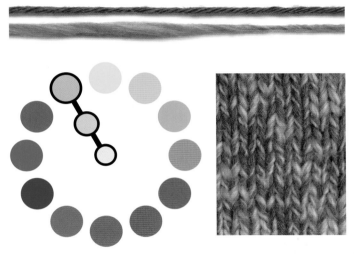

Choose a yarn color and then pair it with a darker or lighter shade of that same color. Knitting a variegated slubbed green wool yarn with a darker solid green wool yarn creates a monochromatic effect.

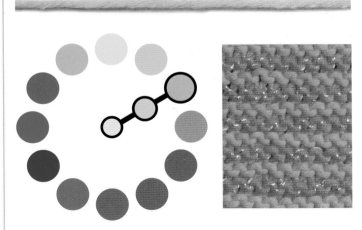

Solid-cotton orange yarn is knit with a lighter orange (apricot) cotton yarn for a balanced, bright combination.

ANALOGOUS YARNS

Analogous color yarns provide the most visually pleasing combinations. Use one or two primary colors and two or more consecutive colors that are next to each other on the color wheel. Examples of analogous color combinations are yellow + yellow-orange + orange, orange + red-orange + red, red + red-violet + violet, violet + blue-violet + blue, and blue + blue-green + green.

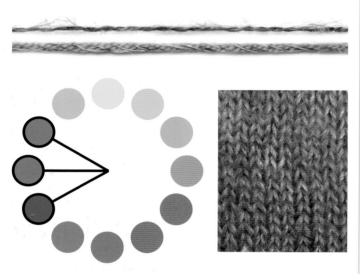

Combine colorful and textural analogous yarns. A solid green cotton blend is knit with a variegated blue-violet mohair.

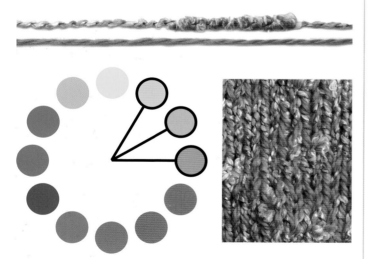

An analogous bouclé slubbed yarn is knit with a solid rust wool blend. This softens the surface texture of the uneven bouclé without changing the color.

COMPLEMENTARY YARNS

Use yarns of complementary (opposite) colors as a way of enhancing color and creating vibrant effects. These colors are easy to recognize, as they lie on opposite sides of the color wheel. Examples of complementary colors are yellow + violet, red + green, and blue + orange.

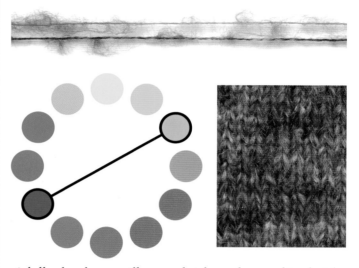

A dull-colored yarn will appear brighter when combined with a darker complementary-color yarn. This variegated orange mohair yarn looks more colorful when knit with a darker blue variegated mohair yarn.

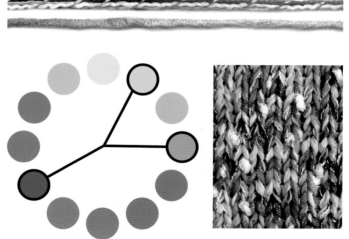

Split-complementary color combinations offer more variety and effects. Choose one color from one side of the color wheel and two opposite colors that lie on either side of the other complementary color. Monochromatic variegated blue yarn is knit with variegated yellow-orange-red for a dramatic texture.

BLACK AND WHITE YARNS

Knitting a black or white yarn together with a colored yarn is an easy and effective way to enhance the color. When you combine a pastel yarn with light gray yarn, the pastel looks brighter. Yarn colors appear more vivid when knit with black or dark gray.

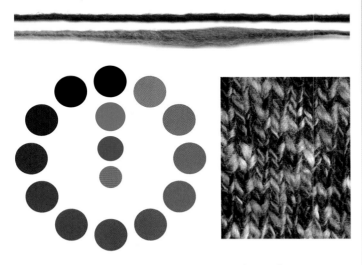

Brighten the color of a striped or variegated yarn by mixing it with a medium gray or black yarn. A muted blue-violet slubbed wool yarn gives the impression of being brighter when knit together with a black wool yarn.

Combining a bright yarn with a white or light gray will make it appear lighter. Create a light blue effect with a bright blue wool yarn knit with a fuzzy wool-blend white yarn.

NEUTRAL YARNS

When we think of neutral colors we usually just think of beige. There are many variations of neutral, however, that range from tan to terra cotta. Neutral yarns are safe color choices that mix well with many yarn colors. Warm neutral colors are a section of the color wheel from yellow-green to red. Cool neutral colors are a section of the color wheel from green to red-violet.

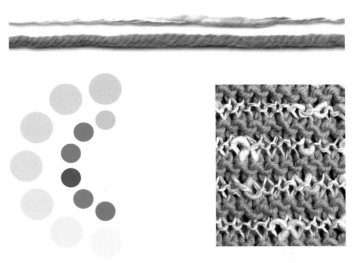

To neutralize a color, knit cool neutrals with cool yarn colors, and warm neutrals with warm yarn colors. A solid green wool yarn is knit with a cool slubbed yarn for a textural blend.

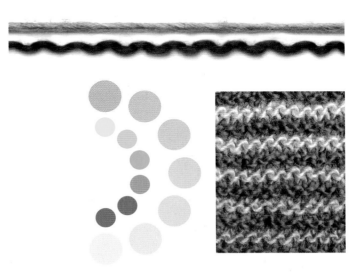

For contrasting neutral combinations, knit cool neutrals with warm yarn colors, and warm neutrals with cool yarn colors. A warm variegated wool yarn is knit together with solid navy blue wool. The warm neutral yarn enhances the color and brightness of the navy yarn.

3
HOW TO
SUBSTITUTE YARNS

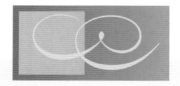

Selecting the proper substitution yarn is often a daunting task. It is estimated that 34 percent of knitters choose to substitute yarns in a commercial pattern. The aim of this chapter is to guide the beginning knitter in narrowing down the search for the best substitution yarn. The guidelines provided here will assist you in making the optimum yarn selection. ✳ Important factors to consider when selecting a substitution yarn include weight similarity, gauge consistency, fiber compatibility, yarn characteristics, stitch definition, and yardage. The information provided in this chapter will eliminate the hassle of selecting a substitution yarn for your next project. You will save time and money, and your finished garment will look great and fit properly.

LET'S GET STARTED

Finding the right substitution yarn does not have to be a daunting experience that takes all the fun and excitement out of your knitting project. You'll find that most yarn shops will carry other yarns with a weight, fiber, and gauge similar to those of the original yarn specified in the pattern.

There are many reasons for substituting yarns. Typically, knitwear designers confirm with yarn manufacturers that the yarn they are specifying is not scheduled to be discontinued. However, due to style trends and seasonal sales, some yarns will inevitably be discontinued. While yarn shop owners stock their favorite, best-selling brands, not all brands are featured.

Sometimes the cost of the yarn can be a prohibitive factor, especially for a project that requires several skeins, such as a sweater or coat. A variety of yarn blends are available, so substituting a lower-priced yarn is an economical way to modify a pattern that you will love to knit.

Color is a personal choice. But what if you don't like the colorways specified in the pattern, or the store doesn't carry all the colors you need? Colors are also seasonal. It's important to find the color that is right for your project. You may prefer a color of a different brand than the one specified in the pattern.

Many people have allergic reactions to wool. However, processing, coloring dyes, or the environment in which the yarn is stored may also cause adverse reactions. Sometimes people who are allergic to wool can tolerate pure non-allergenic alpaca yarn. In addition, even though you may not be allergic, the itchiness of the yarn fibers may give you reason to substitute a yarn.

Whether you change yarn due to personal preference or necessity, finding the right replacement yarn will determine the success of your knitted project, especially when you are knitting a garment. Before you start your search to find a substitute yarn, note the specifications of the original yarn in the pattern.

The beginner knitter must be mindful of several important reasons for substituting yarns. To make a successful, well-informed decision, you should consider weight, gauge, fiber, yarn characteristics, stitch definition, and yardage when selecting a replacement.

YARN WEIGHT

The weight or thickness of the yarn is an important factor to consider when selecting a substitute. For best results, select a yarn weight that matches the weight of the yarn in the pattern. Yarns are divided into super fine, fine, light, medium, bulky, and super bulky weights. If the pattern shows the standard yarn weight symbol (1 through 6) for the yarn, find a replacement yarn in that weight.

If you do not know the original yarn weight, use the ball band gauge of the yarn in the pattern. Several yarn manufacturers' websites or other websites list ball band information, including www.yarndex.com and www.wiseneedle.com. When you find the gauge, consult the chart below or www.yarnstandards.com. The chart will narrow your search for a replacement yarn. Your individual knitting tension may require you to select a different needle size to obtain the specific gauge in the pattern. Remember, you are knitting an original garment and your knitting tension may need to be adjusted to fit the pattern you are following.

Standard Yarn Weight System
Yarn Weight 1 – Super Fine: *Sock, Fingering, Baby* Knit Gauge Range: Stockinette Stitch to 4 inches • 27–32 sts Needle Size: Metric 2.25–3.25mm Needle Size: US 1–3
Yarn Weight 2 – Fine: *Sport, Baby* Knit Gauge Range: Stockinette Stitch to 4 inches • 23–26 sts Needle Size: Metric 3.25–3.75mm Needle Size: US 3–5
Yarn Weight 3 – Light: *DK (Double Knit), Light Worsted* Knit Gauge Range: Stockinette Stitch to 4 inches • 21–24 sts Needle Size: Metric 3.75–4.5mm Needle Size: US 5–7
Yarn Weight 4 – Medium: *Worsted, Afghan, Aran* Knit Gauge Range: Stockinette Stitch to 4 inches • 16–20 sts Needle Size: Metric 4.5–5.5mm Needle Size: US 7–9
Yarn Weight 5 – Bulky: *Chunky, Craft, Rug* Knit Gauge Range: Stockinette Stitch to 4 inches • 12–15 sts Needle Size: Metric 5.5–8mm Needle Size: US 9–11
Yarn Weight 6 – Super Bulky: *Bulky, Roving* Knit Gauge Range: Stockinette Stitch to 4 inches • 6–11 sts Needle Size: Metric 8mm and up Needle Size: 11 and up

GAUGE

Gauge is just as important as weight when choosing a substitution yarn. The importance of gauge cannot be overstated. But which gauge do you match—the pattern gauge or the original ball band gauge? Initially, you'll need to find a yarn that is the same as or very similar to the gauge from the ball band of the yarn in the pattern. You probably don't have the ball band since you are substituting the yarn. This information may be found in knit shops, on yarn manufacturers' websites, or websites that list "yarn by gauge," including www.yarndex.com and www.wiseneedle.com. To find the best replacement yarn possible, use the needle size specified in the pattern, matched with the stitch gauge and row gauge of the original yarn.

Once you find a substitute yarn, you'll then want to knit the same gauge as in the pattern. Knit a 5-inch by 5-inch (larger than normal) test swatch with the specified needles and recommended stitch pattern so that you can see how the yarn works. It's important to match the stitch and row gauge listed in the pattern, but the needle size is only a suggestion. This is why patterns often list the needle size with a note: "or size to obtain gauge." If your knit swatch is too large, use smaller needles. If your knit swatch is too small, change to larger needles. You may need to experiment with different sizes of needles until your knitting tension matches the pattern gauge. The exact number of stitches and rows will predict the precise measurements of the garment you are knitting.

Here's where the fun begins. All knitters work at a different tension—how loose or how tight your individual stitches are on the needle. Most knitters prefer knitting a fitted garment. Your individual knitting tension will have a direct effect on the size and fit of the garment you are knitting. Let's consider a pattern that calls for 4 stitches per inch (16 stitches per 4 inches). If the finished garment measures 20 inches wide, you would have exactly 80 stitches when completed. However, if you are knitting 5 stitches per inch and you divide 80 by 5, your finished garment will measure only 16 inches wide and will be too small. We highly recommend that you never begin knitting a garment without first making a 5-inch by 5-inch swatch and blocking it to test the accuracy of your knitting. Finding the correct yarn gauge for your substitute yarn will ensure the comfort and fit of the finished garment you are knitting.

FIBER

Once you determine the original weight of the yarn specified in the pattern, finding the right replacement fiber is essential. Check the fiber content listed on the ball band of the original yarn. The information should be provided in the pattern, or it can be obtained from the manufacturer's website or another reliable online site such as www.yarndex.com. If the yarn is a 100% pure fiber, the best replacement is the same fiber from another manufacturer. If the original yarn is a blend, try to purchase a similar blend so that the yarn will react in the same fashion. A synthetic blend will knit up differently than a 100% pure fiber yarn. If possible, try to determine the ply and finish of the original yarn.

If you are a new knitter, consider the fiber when choosing a pattern. It is better to start out being able to use a yarn that is readily available rather than an expensive, obscure yarn. Cotton and cotton-blend yarns are popular fibers that are available in a wide range of weights. Wool and wool-blend yarns are classic fibers and are widely available in a range of weights and colorways. Depending on the ply and finish, fibers from different manufacturers can knit up differently.

Take into consideration the function of the project when looking for a replacement fiber. If the pattern is a garment, try to get as close as possible to the original yarn fiber specified in the pattern. If the project is a purse, think about the durability of the yarn you are replacing. Will it be strong and sturdy enough for daily use? Does the original pattern yarn need to have some stretch? If the project is a scarf, finding the perfect substitution fiber may not be as critical.

Save time by knitting a test swatch. Every yarn has unique fiber characteristics, which should be considered carefully when choosing a replacement yarn. The individual qualities of the new yarn will ultimately determine the look, fit, and feel of your finished knitwear.

YARN CHARACTERISTICS

There are many yarn characteristics to consider when selecting a substitution yarn. Consider the use and wearability of the knit project. Must the knit fabric have strength, durability, or resilience? Does it need to drape delicately, or be light and lacy? Drape refers to how a fabric falls or holds its shape when worn. Perhaps the knitwear needs elasticity and stretch. To avoid unforeseen knitting problems, we recommend choosing a yarn with a fiber content, weight, and gauge that closely resemble those of the yarn specified in the pattern. To get a better understanding of the yarn you are replacing, look at the photograph of the project. How does the finished knit fabric look? The new fiber may alter the characteristics of the fabric and ultimately the look of the finished garment.

If the yarn is a textural yarn such as bouclé or ribbon, using a plain yarn might alter the appearance of the finished project. When knit, ribbon yarn has a unique elasticity that is difficult to achieve with a completely different yarn. If the pattern uses an angora yarn, and you prefer knitting with an alpaca-merino blend, how will the new fibers affect the stitch definition, softness, and elasticity of the knitted garment? If you are working with a single-ply yarn and want to substitute a multi-ply yarn, great care must be taken in choosing a yarn that will not snag easily, as some have a tendency to do.

The elasticity, or the give of the fabric, is an important characteristic to consider when choosing a replacement yarn. If you are knitting a ribbed or cable pattern, you will need a yarn that has greater elasticity in order to maintain a consistent stitch definition. The elasticity and strength of the replacement yarn are important because they may affect the structure of the finished knitwear.

Finally, the washability factor should be considered when choosing a replacement yarn. Be sure to follow the washing instructions with a test swatch. Some yarns relax and soften when washed in warm water; others may curl around the edges, bleed, stretch, or shrink. A washed and blocked test swatch will eliminate any guesswork regarding the new yarn.

STITCH DEFINITION

Most commercial patterns provide specifications that include the yarn gauge, needle size, and stitch patterns used to knit the garment. We have discussed the criteria for choosing a substitution yarn, but you should also consider the effects of the replacement yarn on the stitch definition in the pattern. The goal is to select a fiber that will not drastically alter the appearance of the finished garment.

The effect should be minimal if you're working in garter or stockinette stitch patterns. However, if the pattern calls for seed, rib, moss, cable, or complex stitch patterns—such as diamond, popcorn stitches or intarsia—we recommend that you knit a test swatch and compare the look and texture of the new yarn with the original pattern picture.

Knit a test gauge swatch to compare the overall effect on the stitch pattern, especially when working with a different yarn fiber. Different fibers may alter the final appearance of the stitch pattern, and this will become very apparent in your test swatch. Natural fibers such as wool, mohair, angora, and alpaca are lightweight, soft, and generally more expensive. They are often spun with other fibers to reduce cost. Synthetic fibers such as acrylic, polyester, and others are less expensive and are usually machine washable. All these fibers will affect the performance of the yarn differently, and their individual characteristics must be weighed carefully when choosing a substitution yarn.

An informed knitter who considers gauge, weight, fiber compatibility, yarn characteristics, and stitch definition will be highly successful in choosing a substitution yarn. Your finished garment will look good, fit properly, and give you a great sense of accomplishment.

YARDAGE

Since yarn comes in a variety of lengths, an important calculation to consider is the amount of substitution yarn needed to complete a project. Generally, manufacturers provide the ball, skein, or hank yardage information on every ball band. Commercial patterns also give the knitter information regarding the number of balls needed to complete the project.

The number of balls, skeins, or hanks needed can be determined easily by doing a simple calculation. If the pattern you are following calls for 2 balls of yarn at 200 yards (185m) per ball, you would need 400 yards (370m) to complete the project. If the replacement yarn has 100 yards (92m) per ball, simply calculate 400 yards (370m) ÷ 100 yards (92m). You would need 4 balls of yarn to complete the project. Always round the yardage amount off to the next whole number and allow extra yardage for joining strands.

If you have a ball of yarn with no ball band, you'll need to determine the yardage on the ball. Here's a simple solution. Cut a 3-yard (2.75m) strand and weigh it on a scale that measures ounces; a digital postage scale works well. After determining the weight of the strand, weigh the ball of yarn. Divide the weight of the ball of yarn by the weight of the strand. For example, if the 3-yard (2.75m) strand weighs 2 ounces and the ball weighs 50 ounces, therefore 50 ÷ 2 = 25 pieces that measure 3 yds (2.75m) each. Multiply 25 (pieces) x 3 yards (2.75m) = 75 yards (69m) on the ball of yarn. Correctly calculating the amount of yarn needed to complete a project saves money and guarantees that you will not run out of yarn before completing the garment.

KNITTING 2 STRANDS TOG

Knitting two strands together offers many colorful, textural, and functional possibilities. Experiment with swatches and create your own combinations. Examples include the following:

- Tone down a variegated yarn by pairing it with a solid matching color.
- Add texture by knit mixing a smooth-ply worsted yarn with a bouclé yarn.
- Knit two strands together to add strength and durability when knitting a purse strap or gusset.
- Bulk up a sweater with a double worsted yarn in place of a bulky yarn.
- Combine a fingering yarn with the main yarn to add color and sparkle to your knitting without affecting the gauge.

Making the gauge work with doubled yarn requires a test swatch. Below is a list of yarn weights and their matching double-strand weights.

- Fingering doubled = sport
- Sport or DK doubled = worsted
- Worsted doubled = bulky

Knitting with two separate yarn balls can be tricky. Often when you are winding two yarns together they will not wind at the same rate or they may slide. When you are working with two yarn balls, keeping them separated will prevent tangling. Placing the yarn balls in separate bags makes them easier to handle. Make sure the care instructions are similar so that the yarns react in the same way when washed or blocked. Not all yarns work perfectly when knit together. Knitting yarns of a similar weight together achieves the best results. Knit two strands together or try knitting alternate rows of two different strands in your preferred stitch pattern.

A fuzzier or thicker yarn might dominate the combination. Pairing mohair with chenille will result in a blurred effect on the stitches. Knitting two yarns together that don't have much stretch can cause them to bind. However, you can combine yarns to your advantage to create more exciting and colorful knitting combinations. Chapter 4, Yarn Harmony Pairings (page 34), features 275 seasonal swatches in five essential yarn fibers and five different textural yarns in six different color formats. It's fun and enlightening to see which yarns work best together.

4
YARN HARMONY PAIRINGS

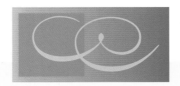

Explore more than 275 color pairing swatches using ten fabulous yarn types, (five basic fiber yarns and five textural yarns) cotton, bamboo, silk, mohair, wool, ribbon, bouclé, chenille, slubbed, and multi-strand. They are shown in six colors within six different color relationships, using 200 strands of yarn knit in two distinct stitch patterns. Each swatch was knit with a needle size corresponding to the yarn using the standard yarn weight system. For example, light/DK weight yarn was knit using needles sized US 5–7 (3.75–4.5mm), and worsted/medium weight yarn was knit using needles sized US 7–9 (4.5–5.5mm). ✳ Each spread showcases six stockinette stitch swatches knit with two strands together and six garter stitch swatches knit with single strands in row-by-row striping. Since yarn changes seasonally, this chapter is divided into four sections: spring, summer, fall, and winter. Each seasonal color range represents a color palette for that season in the six major color groups: yellow, orange, red, violet, blue, and green. ✳ This chapter is an essential starting point for choosing fashion yarn colors. You can apply these combinations to your own patterns. As a bonus, there are eight patterns featuring pairings from each season. There are no rules against wearing colors in other seasons. Refer to the palette of colors for your specific style preference. You'll discover the infinite possibilities of pairing yarns, and you'll enjoy knitting your own fashion combinations.

SPRING PAIRINGS

The spring pairings display a beautiful array of pastel yarns. These soft, seasonal colors include pale and chiffon yellows, salmon and coral oranges, pink and rose reds, lavender and lilac purples, powder and ice blues, and light citrus and mint greens. The spring fine to light weight yarn swatches include cotton, bamboo, and silk yarns in bouclé, ribbon, and multi-strand textures. The Spring Purse and Scarf patterns each represent two pairings in this section. The Spring Scarf *(page 51)* is knit with soft complementary blue cotton ribbon and red and orange bamboo yarns *(page 46)*. Monochromatic pink ribbon and cotton yarn colors *(page 42)* blend beautifully in the Spring Purse *(page 50)* to create a durable texture and stylish fashion accessory. The spring pairings afford a rainbow of pleasing pastels that reflect the essence of spring.

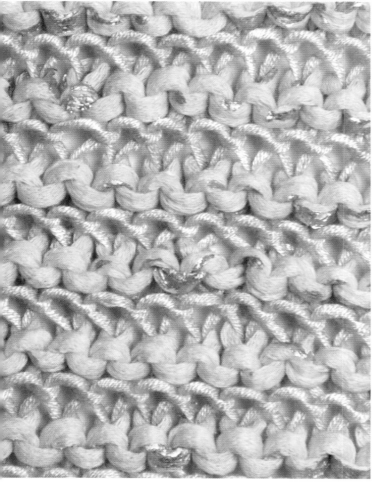

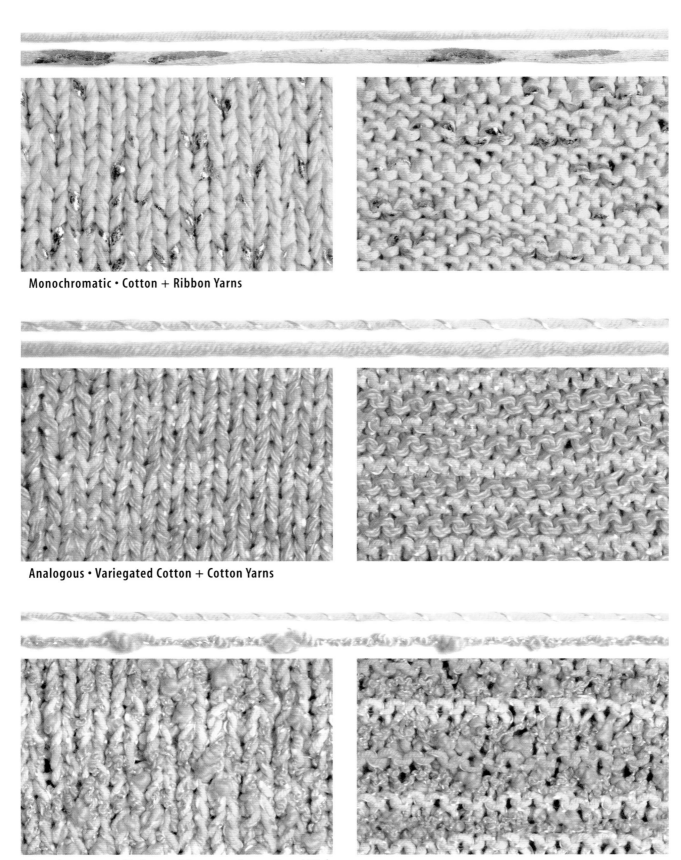

Monochromatic • Cotton + Ribbon Yarns

Analogous • Variegated Cotton + Cotton Yarns

Complementary • Variegated Cotton + Cotton Bouclé Yarns

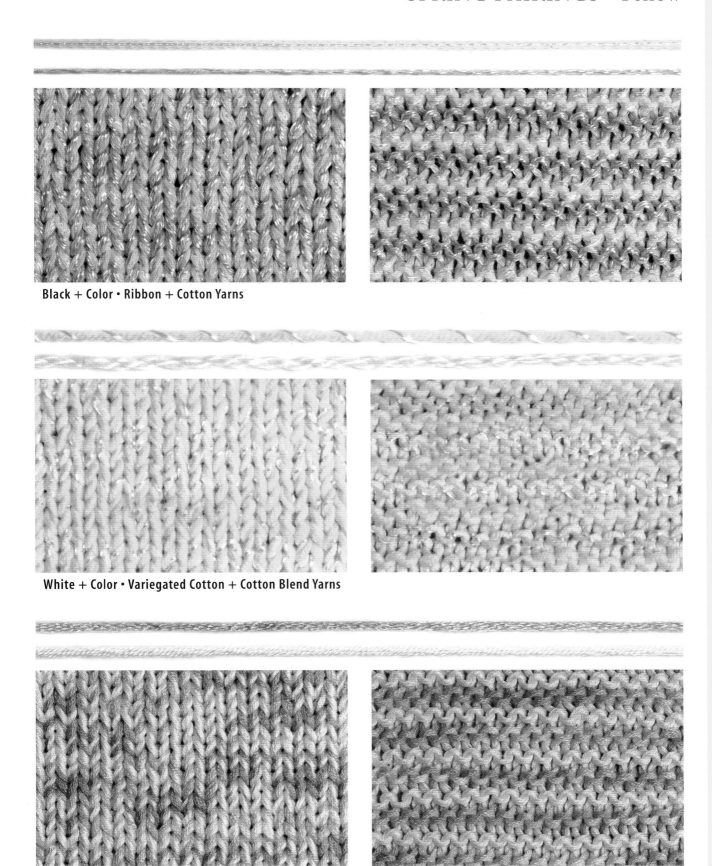

Black + Color • Ribbon + Cotton Yarns

White + Color • Variegated Cotton + Cotton Blend Yarns

Neutral + Color • Variegated Cotton + Cotton Yarns

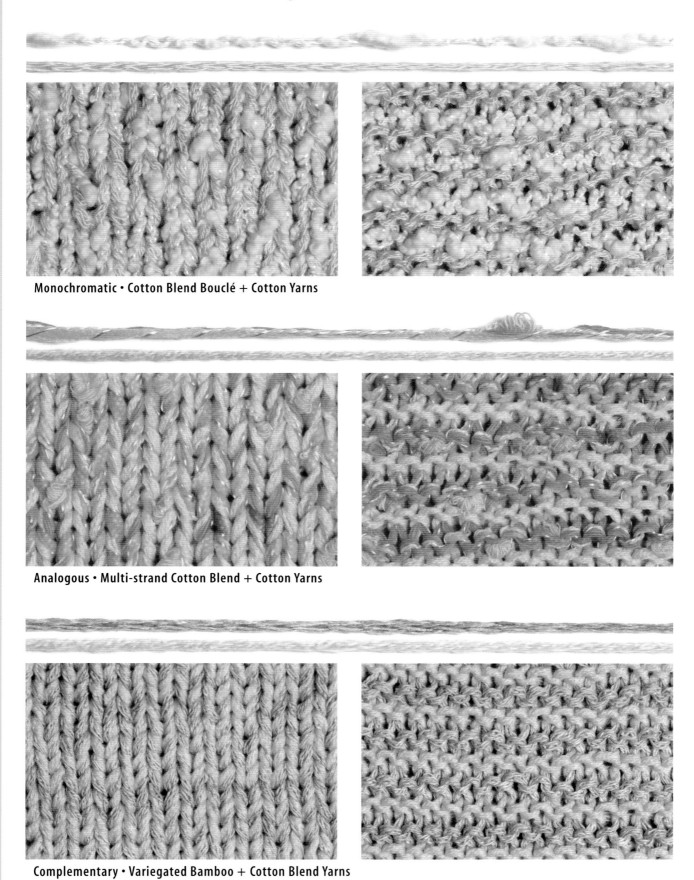

Monochromatic • Cotton Blend Bouclé + Cotton Yarns

Analogous • Multi-strand Cotton Blend + Cotton Yarns

Complementary • Variegated Bamboo + Cotton Blend Yarns

Black + Color • Cotton + Multi-strand Cotton Blend Yarns

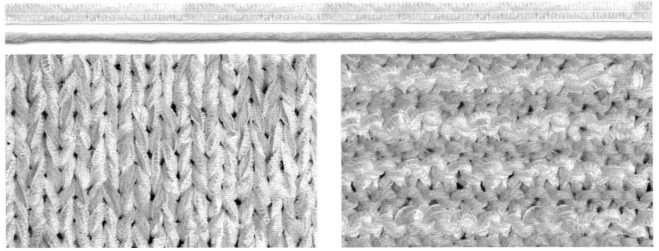

White + Color • Ribbon + Bamboo Yarns

Neutral + Color • Cotton Blend + Cotton Yarns

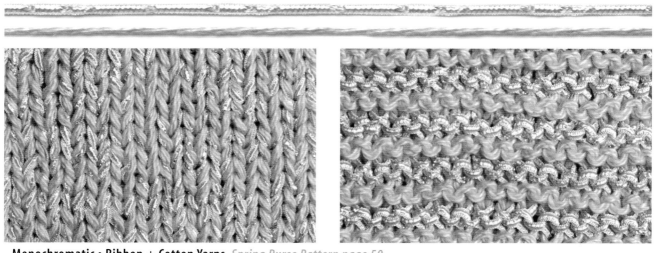

Monochromatic • Ribbon + Cotton Yarns, *Spring Purse Pattern page 50*

Analogous • Multi-strand Cotton Blend + Cotton Blend Yarns

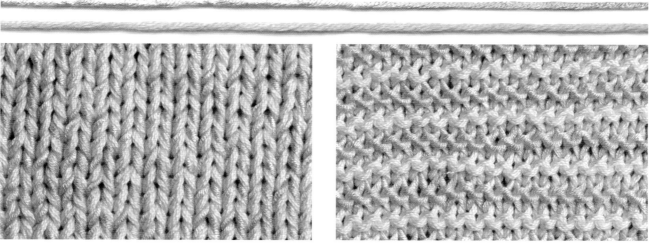

Complementary • Variegated Bamboo + Cotton Yarns

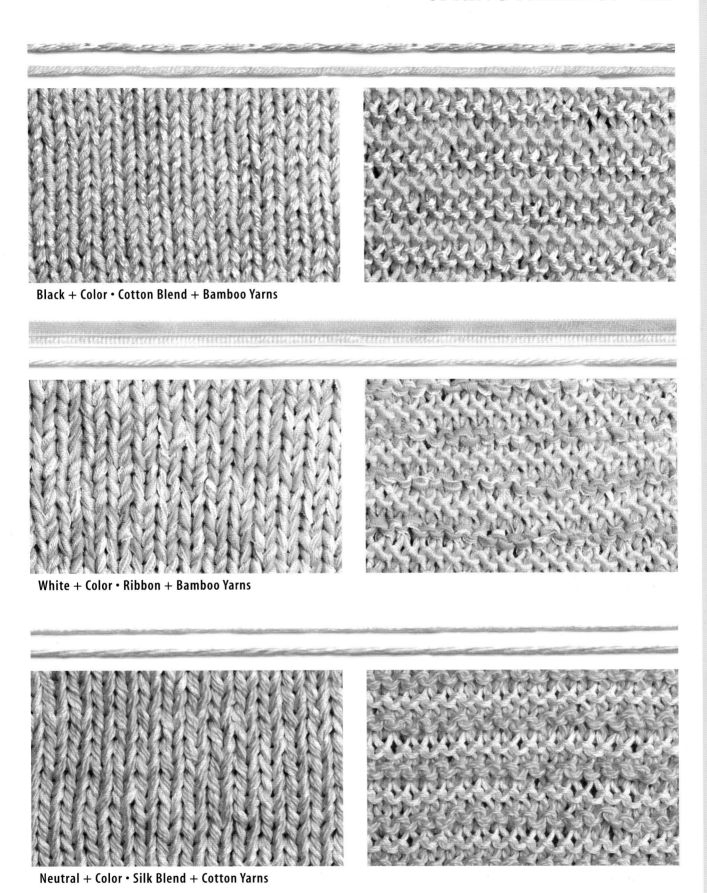

Black + Color • Cotton Blend + Bamboo Yarns

White + Color • Ribbon + Bamboo Yarns

Neutral + Color • Silk Blend + Cotton Yarns

Monochromatic • Cotton + Cotton Blend Yarns

Analogous • Cotton + Cotton Blend Yarns

Complementary • Cotton + Cotton Blend Bouclé Yarns

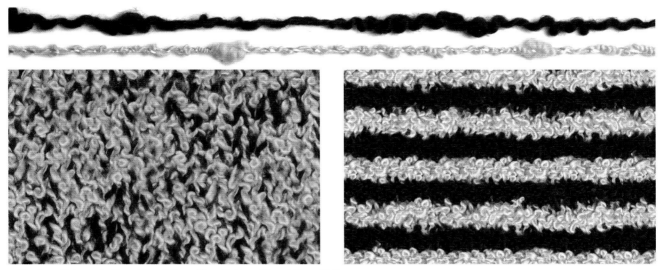

Black + Color • Cotton Blend Bouclé + Cotton Blend Bouclé Yarns

White + Color • Cotton + Cotton Blend Yarns

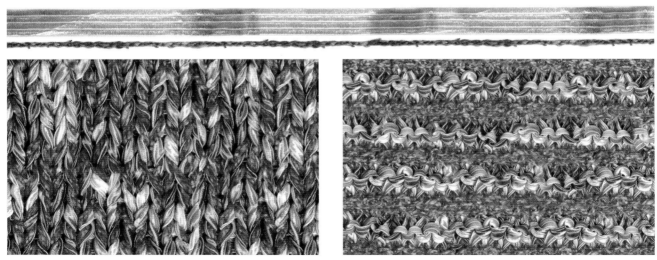

Neutral + Color • Ribbon + Cotton Yarns

Monochromatic • Cotton + Bamboo Yarns

Analogous • Multi-strand Cotton Blend + Cotton Yarns

Complementary • Variegated Bamboo + Ribbon Yarns, *Spring Scarf Pattern page 51*

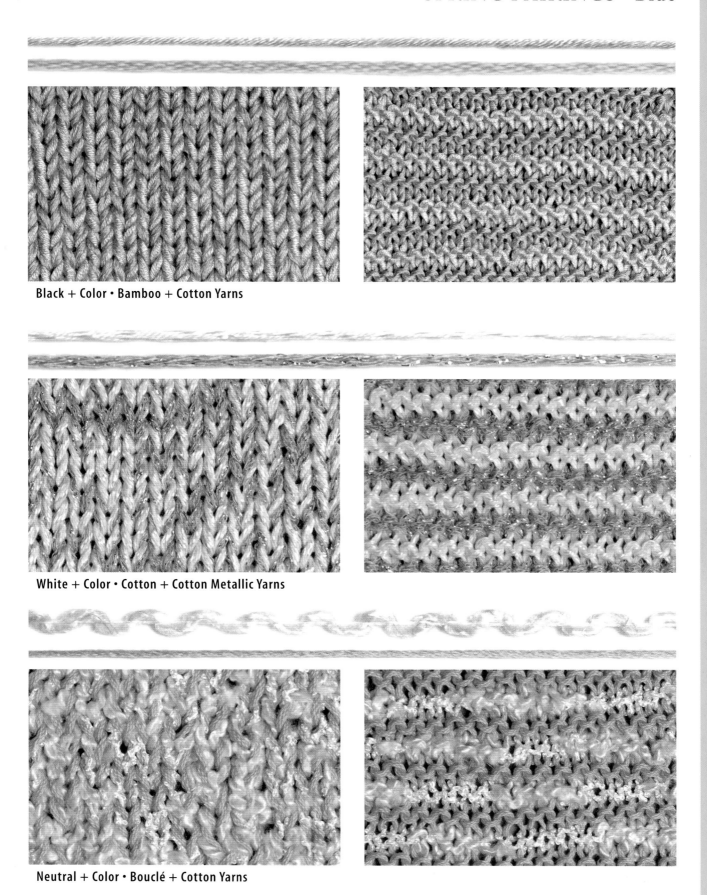

Black + Color • Bamboo + Cotton Yarns

White + Color • Cotton + Cotton Metallic Yarns

Neutral + Color • Bouclé + Cotton Yarns

Monochromatic • Cotton Blend Slub + Twisted Cotton Yarns

Analogous • Cotton + Bamboo Yarns

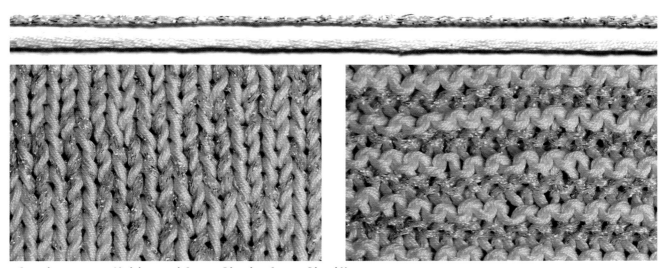

Complementary • Multi-strand Cotton Blend + Cotton Blend Yarns

Black + Color • Cotton + Cotton Blend Yarns

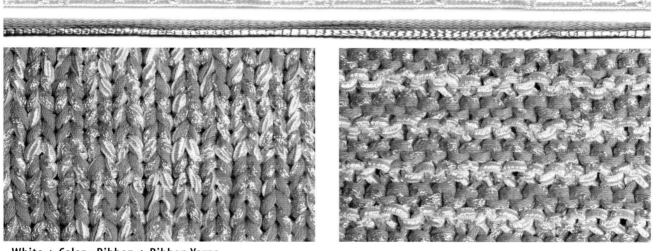

White + Color • Ribbon + Ribbon Yarns

Neutral + Color • Cotton + Cotton Yarns

SPRING PURSE

Two monochromatic pink yarns are paired together to create this lovely Spring Purse. A thin ribbon accent yarn is blended with a base cotton yarn that adds sparkle and texture. The handmade glass button and I-cord complete the design. This striking purse is ideal for casual as well as dressy occasions.

FRONT AND BACK (ONE PIECE)

With US 10 needles and 1 strand of A and 1 strand of B held tog, CO 36 sts.

Work 3 rows in Garter st.

Work in St st for 6" (15cm).

BOTTOM

Work in Reverse St st for 3" (7.5cm).

BACK

Work in St st for 6" (15cm).

Work 4 rows in Garter st.

RIBBED FLAP

Change to US 4 needles. With B only, P1, work in 2 x 2 Ribbing patt to last st, P1.

Next Row: (WS) K1, work in 2 x 2 Ribbing patt to last st, K1.

Repeat last 2 rows until flap measures 4" (10cm).

BO loosely.

FLAP EDGING

With the RS facing, and with US 4 needles and A only, pick up and K 12 sts down the left side edge, 36 sts across the bottom edge, and 12 sts up the right side edge. (60 sts)

Work 3 rows in Garter st.

BO loosely.

I-CORD HANDLE

With US 8 double-pointed needles and A and B held tog, CO 3 sts. Work the I-cord for 18" (45.75 cm).

BO.

FINISHING

Fold the bag in half with the RS facing. With A and B held tog, sew the side seams. With A and B held tog, make a 1" (2.5cm) loop and attach it to the WS of the flap. Attach the D rings to the inside side seams 2 rows below the BO edge. Sew the I-cord to the D rings. Sew the button to the RS of the front. Place purse insert in bottom of bag.

Carrie A. Sullivan

EASY

YARN

A: 1 ball Louisa Harding Yarns *Glisten* 93yds (85m) / 50g (97% nylon 3% polyester) Color: 07

B: 1 ball Louisa Harding Yarns *Nautical Cotton* 93yds (85m) / 50g (100% mercerized cotton) Color: 03

NEEDLES

US 10 (6mm) and US 4 (3.5mm) straight needles and US 8 (5mm) double-pointed needles, or size needed to obtain gauge.

GAUGE

15 sts and 20 rows = 4" (10cm) with 1 strand of A and 1 strand of B held together over Stockinette stitch patt using size US 10 needles.

FINISHED MEASUREMENTS

9.5" (24cm) wide x 6.5" (16.5cm) high

FINISHING MATERIALS

1 glass button

2 small D rings

Purse insert (Bag-E-Bottom, Size E)

YARN HARMONY PAIRING PAGE 42

SCHEMATICS PAGE 100

Spring Scarf

This light and breezy Spring Scarf combines soft blue ribbon and smooth silky bamboo in a blend of complementary pastel yarns. The design incorporates a series of simple garter stitch rows followed by openwork lace stitches. The scarf is folded and sewn together to create a slender fashion accessory. This uniquely shaped scarf is sure to be a favorite accessory for many occasions.

Scarf
With A and US 10 needles, CO 14 sts.

Rows 1–4: K across.

Row 5: Change to B and US 7 needles, K across.

Row 6: K2, P10, K2.

Row 7: K1, K2tog, (K1, YO) 2x, K2tog 2x, (K1, YO) 2x, K2tog, K1.

Row 8: K across.

Rows 9–20: Repeat Rows 5–8 three more times.

Repeat Rows 1–20 until scarf measures 76" (193cm).

Work Rows 1–4 one more time.

BO loosely.

Finishing
Fold the scarf in half lengthwise and sew the sides tog at sections with A.

Fringe
Cut 24 strands 9" (23cm) long of A, and 8 strands 9" (23cm) long of B. Using 3 pieces of A and 1 piece of B per fringe, work 4 fringes evenly across the CO edge and work 4 fringes evenly across the BO edge. Trim evenly.

Kathleen Greco and Carrie A. Sullivan

BEGINNER

Yarn
A: 2 balls Rowan *Glimmer Print* 44yds (40m) / 50g (50% cotton, 50% acrylic) Color: 004
B: 1 ball Plymouth Yarns *Royal Bamboo* 93yds (86m) / 50g (100% bamboo) Color: 21

Needles
US 10 (6mm) and US 7 (4.50mm) needles, or size needed to obtain gauge.

Gauge
No gauge needed.

Finished Measurements
2" (5cm) wide x 77" (195.5cm) long

Yarn Harmony Pairing page 46

Schematics page 100

SUMMER PAIRINGS

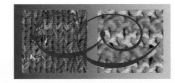

The summer pairings present a vibrant variety of yarn colors. These bright seasonal colors include lemon yellows, bright oranges, magenta and crimson reds, orchid and violet purples, cyan and aqua blues, and lime and chartreuse greens. The fine to medium weight yarn swatches include cotton, bamboo, and silk yarns in bouclé, slubbed, ribbon, and multi-strand textures. �֎ The Summer Sarong and Top patterns each represent two pairings in this section. The Summer Sarong *(page 67)* is knit with bright analogous blue, green, and orange cotton yarns *(page 64)*. Complementary red cotton and variegated ribbon yarns *(page 58)* are combined in the Summer Top *(page 66)*. The textured top uses two strands held together, while the body is worked in a solid red breezy openwork pattern. The passion of summer is well represented by the warm sizzling color pairings.

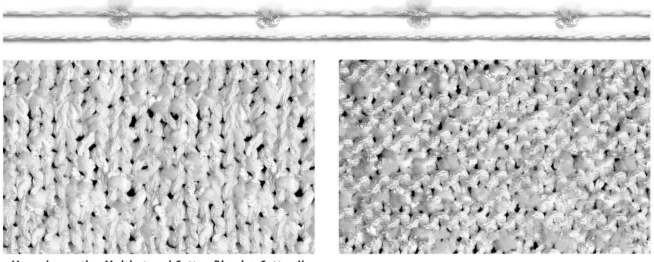

Monochromatic • Multi-strand Cotton Blend + Cotton Yarns

Analogous • Variegated Ribbon + Cotton Yarns

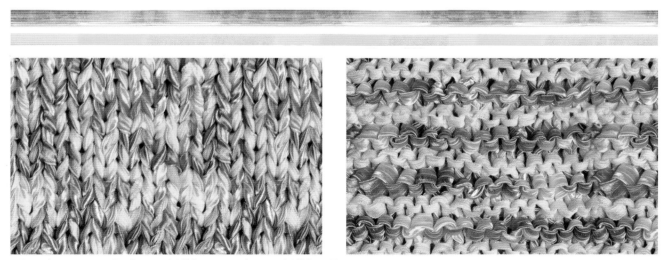

Complementary • Variegated Ribbon + Variegated Ribbon Yarns

Black + Color • Cotton Blend + Cotton Yarns

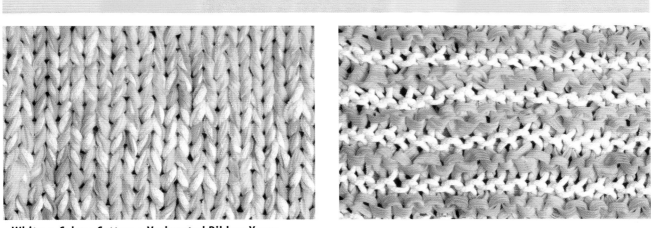

White + Color • Cotton + Variegated Ribbon Yarns

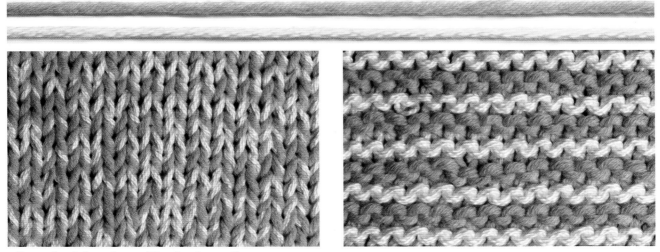

Neutral + Color • Cotton Blend + Cotton Yarns

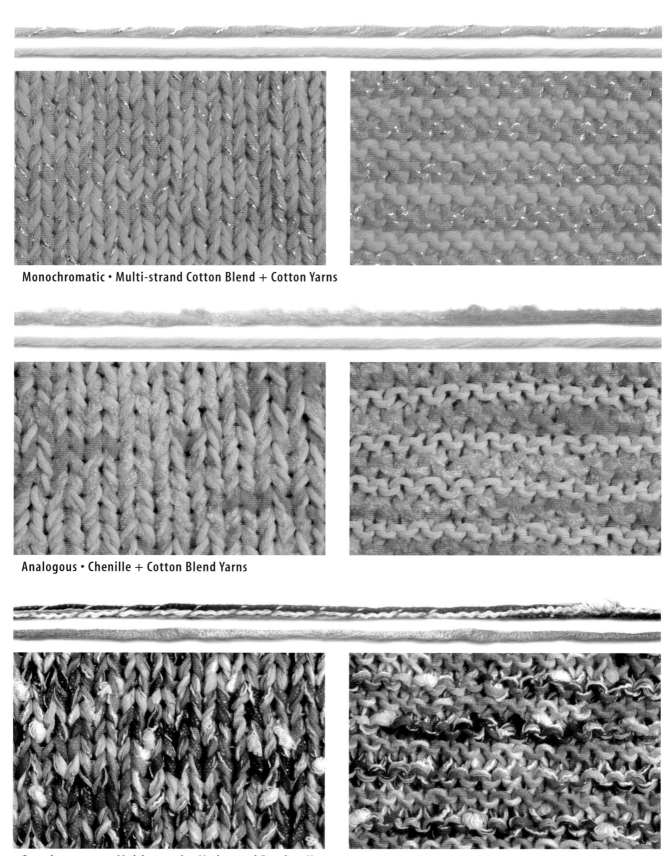

Monochromatic • Multi-strand Cotton Blend + Cotton Yarns

Analogous • Chenille + Cotton Blend Yarns

Complementary • Multi-strand + Variegated Bamboo Yarns

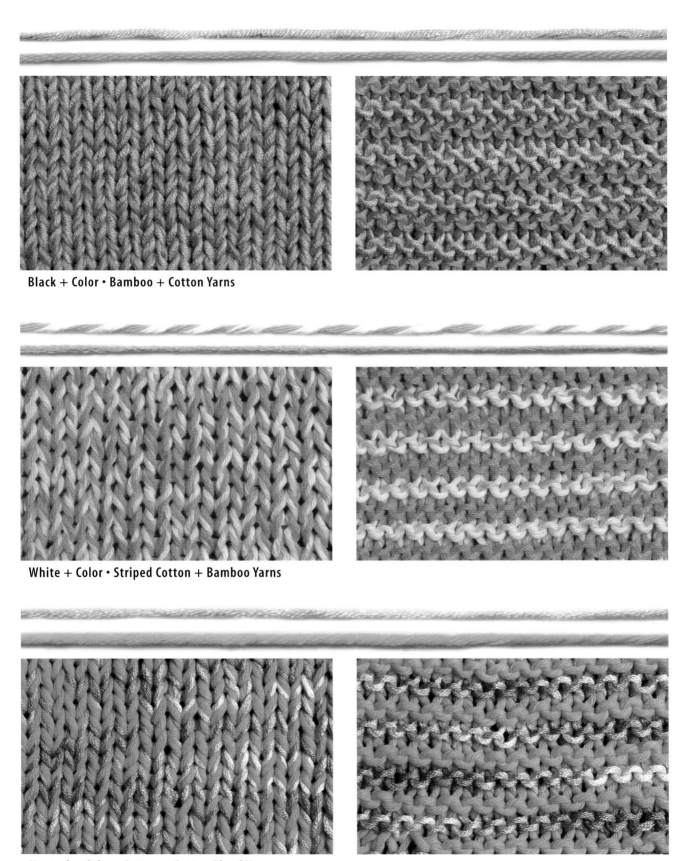

Black + Color • Bamboo + Cotton Yarns

White + Color • Striped Cotton + Bamboo Yarns

Neutral + Color • Cotton + Cotton Blend Yarns

Monochromatic • Ribbon + Cotton Yarns

Analogous • Variegated Cotton + Cotton Blend Yarns

Complementary • Variegated Ribbon + Cotton Yarns, *Summer Top Pattern page 66*

Black + Color • Bamboo + Cotton Blend Yarns

White + Color • Variegated Cotton + Cotton Blend Yarns

Neutral + Color • Cotton + Cotton Yarns

Monochromatic • Cotton + Cotton Blend Yarns

Analogous • Striped Cotton + Cotton Yarns

Complementary • Ribbon + Cotton Blend Yarns

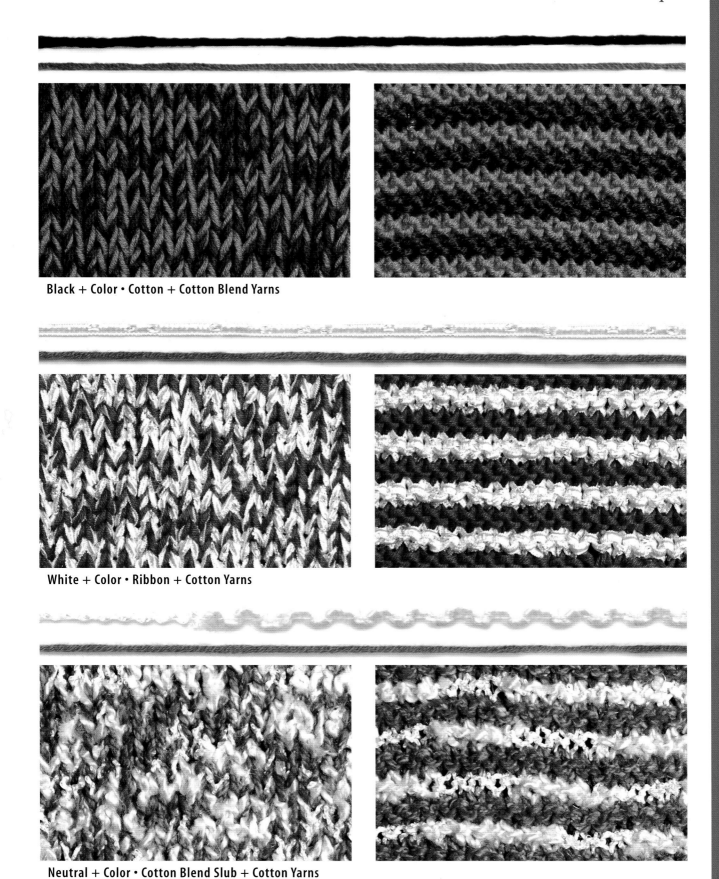

Black + Color • Cotton + Cotton Blend Yarns

White + Color • Ribbon + Cotton Yarns

Neutral + Color • Cotton Blend Slub + Cotton Yarns

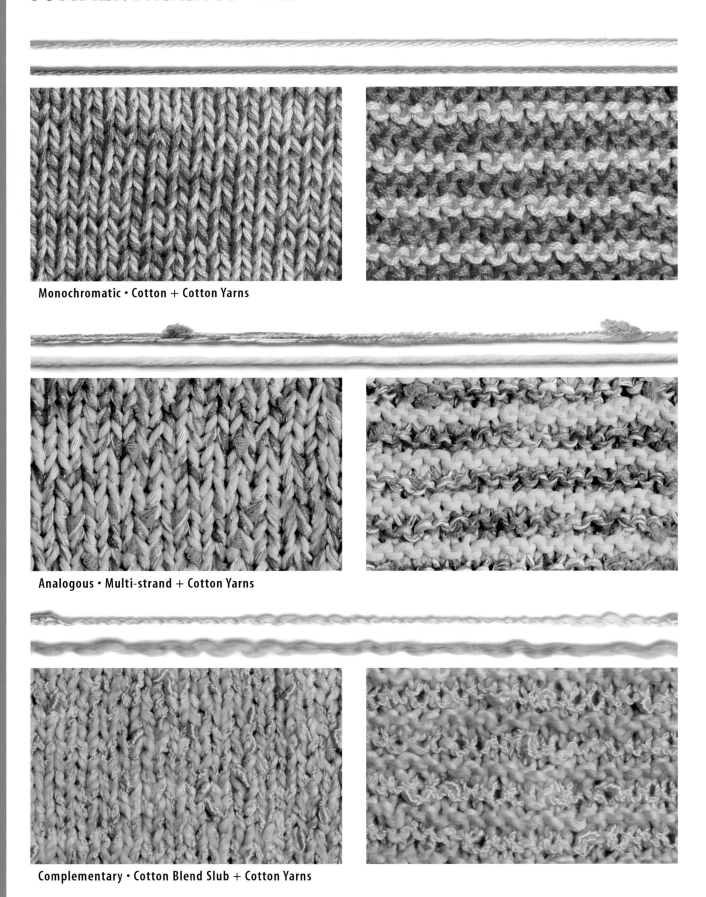

Monochromatic • Cotton + Cotton Yarns

Analogous • Multi-strand + Cotton Yarns

Complementary • Cotton Blend Slub + Cotton Yarns

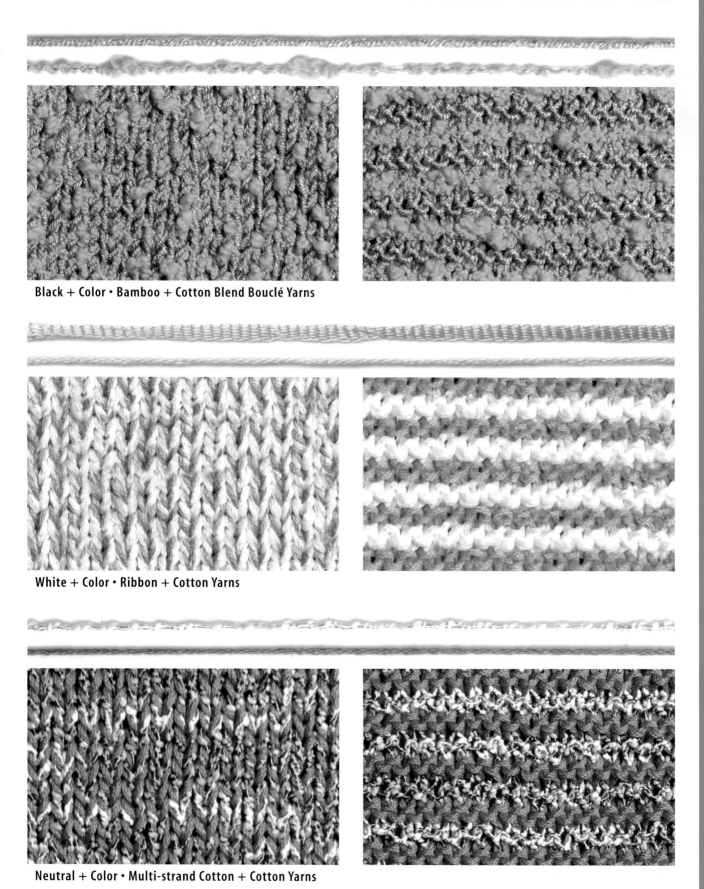

Black + Color • Bamboo + Cotton Blend Bouclé Yarns

White + Color • Ribbon + Cotton Yarns

Neutral + Color • Multi-strand Cotton + Cotton Yarns

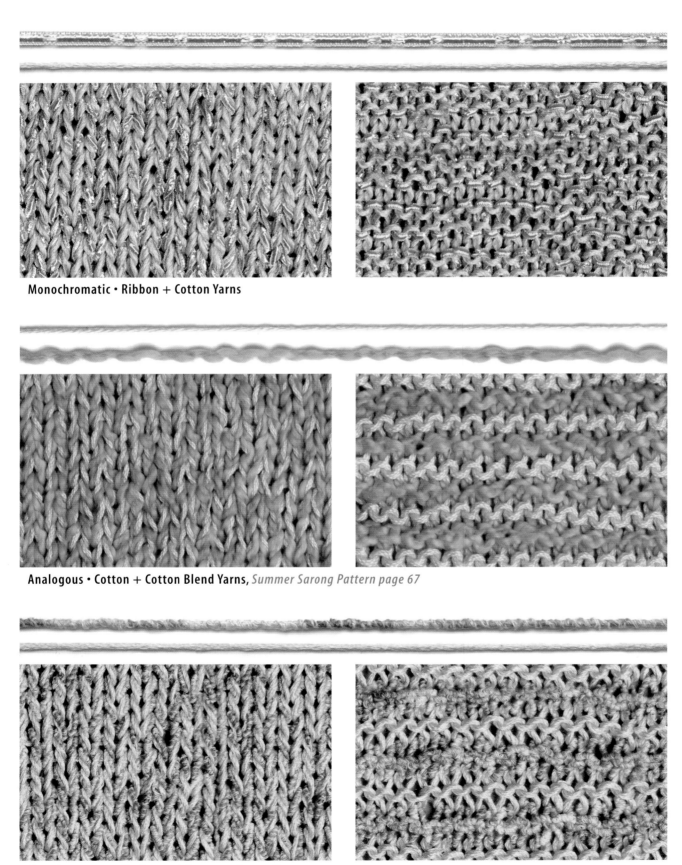

Monochromatic • Ribbon + Cotton Yarns

Analogous • Cotton + Cotton Blend Yarns, *Summer Sarong Pattern page 67*

Complementary • Variegated Cotton + Cotton Yarns

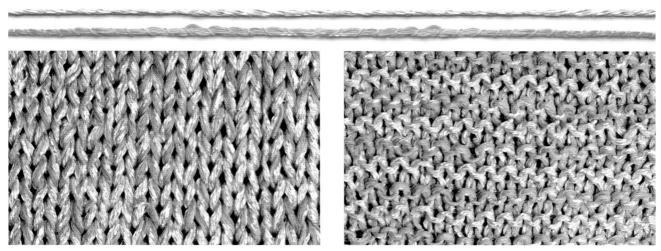

Black + Color • Cotton Blend + Multi-strand Cotton Blend Yarns

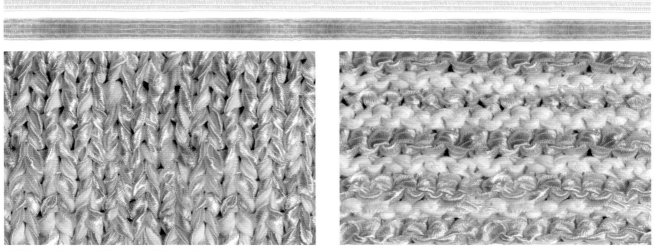

White + Color • Ribbon + Ribbon Yarns

Neutral + Color • Cotton Blend + Cotton Yarns

SUMMER TOP

Be cool in this bright, lightweight Summer Top. An openwork lace pattern is used to knit the simply shaped bodice. Complementary bright red cotton and ribbon yarns paired in a single ribbing pattern provide both elasticity and support. No assembly is needed with this one-piece seamless shell.

FRONT AND BACK (ONE PIECE)

With A, CO 176, 192, 208, 224 sts.

Rnd 1: K around.

Rnd 2: P around.

Rnd 3: PM *(K1, YO) 2x, SKP, [Sl 1-K2tog-PSSO], K2tog, YO, K1, YO, PM, K6*, repeat around.

Rnds 4–6: K around.

Rnds 7–18: Repeat Rnds 3–6 three more times.

Rnd 19: SM *(K1, YO) 2x, SKP, [Sl 1-K2tog-PSSO], K2tog, YO, K1, YO, SM, K4, K2tog*, repeat around. (165, 180, 195, 210 sts)

Rnds 20–22: K around.

Rnd 23: SM *(K1, YO) 2x, SKP, [Sl 1-K2tog-PSSO], K2tog, YO, K1, YO, SM, K5*, repeat around.

Rnds 24–31: Repeat Rnds 20–23 twice.

Rnds 32–34: K around.

Rnd 35: SM *(K1, YO) 2x, SKP, [Sl 1, K2tog-PSSO], K2tog, YO, K1, YO, SM, K2tog, K3*, repeat around. (154, 168, 182, 196 sts)

Rnds 36–38: K around.

Rnd 39: SM *(K1, YO) 2x, SKP, [Sl 1-K2tog-PSSO], K2tog, YO, K1, YO, SM, K4*, repeat around.

Rnds 40–43: Repeat Rnds 36–39 once.

Rnds 44–46: K around.

Rnd 47: SM *(K1, YO) 2x, SKP, [Sl 1-K2tog-PSSO], K2tog, YO, K1, YO, SM, K2, K2tog*, repeat around. (143, 156, 169, 182 sts)

Rnds 48–50: K around.

Rnd 51: SM *(K1, YO) 2x, SKP, [Sl 1-K2tog-PSSO], K2tog, YO, K1, YO, SM, K3*, repeat around.

Rnds 52–58: Repeat Rnds 48–51 twice.

Rnds 59–61: K around.

Rnd 62: Join 1 strand of B and work in 1 x 1 Ribbing patt for 5 (6, 7, 8)" / 12.75 (15.25, 17.75, 20.25) cm, removing markers.

BO loosely.

I-CORD STRAPS

Mark a point on the top edge 3" (8cm) from the left side edge and pick up 3 sts. Knit I-cord 10 (10.5, 11, 11.5) / 25.5 (26.75, 28, 29.25) cm or desired length for the shoulder strap. BO loosely. Mark a point on the top edge 3" (8cm) from the right side edge and repeat for the second strap. Sew the shoulder straps to the back 3" from the side edges.

Kathleen Greco

INTERMEDIATE

YARN

A: 4, 5, 5, 6 balls Plymouth Yarns *Platinum* 99yds (250m) / 50g (50% rayon, 30% nylon, 20% angora) Color: 21

B: 1, 2, 2, 3 balls Katia *Pinta Print* 87yds (221m) / 50g (54% cotton, 46% polyamide) Color: 3904

NEEDLES

US 10.5 (6.5mm) 24" (61cm) circular needles and US 8 (5mm) double-pointed needles, or size needed to obtain gauge.

GAUGE

16 sts and 27 rows = 4" (10cm) with A over Openwork stitch patt using size US 10.5 needles.

18 sts and 20 rows = 4" (10cm) with 1 strand A and 1 strand B held together over 1 x 1 Ribbing stitch patt using size US 10.5 needles.

FINISHED MEASUREMENTS

31.75 (34.75, 37.5, 40.5)" / 80.75 (88.25, 95.25, 102.75) cm wide x 15" (38cm) long

YARN HARMONY PAIRING PAGE 58

SCHEMATICS PAGE 100

SUMMER SARONG

Bright, beautiful hues of blue, green, and orange cotton yarns create this cool Summer Sarong. The warm-weather wrap is knit with openwork drop stitches on large needles. The cotton yarns have different textures and are easy to substitute. This sassy sarong is an ideal, chic cover-up for strolling along the beach or lounging around the pool.

FRONT AND BACK (ONE PIECE)

With A and C held tog, CO 80 sts.

Rows 1–4: K across.

Row 5: K1, K2tog 4x, K to last 9 sts, K2tog 4x, K1. (72 sts)

Row 6: *K1, YO* repeat from * to * across, ending with K1.

Row 7: *K1, drop YO* repeat from * to *, ending with K1.

Row 8: K1, K2tog 2x, K to last 5 sts, K2tog 2x, K1. (68 sts)

Row 9: Repeat Row 6.

Row 10: Repeat Row 7.

Row 11: Repeat Row 8. (64 sts)

Row 12: Repeat Row 6.

Row 13: Repeat Row 7.

Change to A, B, and C held tog.

Rows 14, 17, and 20: Repeat Row 8.

Rows 15, 18, and 21: Repeat Row 6.

Rows 16, 19, and 22: Repeat Row 7. (52 sts)

Change to A and B held tog.

Rows 23, 26, and 29: Repeat Row 8.

Rows 24, 27, and 30: Repeat Row 6.

Rows 25, 28, and 31: Repeat Row 7. (40 sts)

Rows 32–35: K across.

BO loosely.

FINISHING

Using A, cut 36 strands 7" (18cm) long for the fringe. String 3 beads on each end and tie a knot. Starting at first st of CO edge, fold the strand in half, forming a loop, and wrap over st with a slipknot. Working toward the center, repeat every 3 sts along the bottom edge 7 times. Working up right side edge, work every 3 sts 11 times. Repeat for the left side of the sarong. To wear, wrap the sarong around the waist and secure with a shawl pin.

Carrie A. Sullivan

BEGINNER

YARN

A: 2 balls Manos del Uruguay *Cotton Stria* 116yds (107m) / 50g (100% cotton) Color: 210
B: 1 ball Tahki *Cotton Classic* 108yds (99.5m) / 50g (100% cotton) Color: 3723
C: 1 ball Twisted Sister *Oasis* 102yds (94m) / 50g (68% rayon, 32% cotton) Color: Mango

NEEDLES

US 17 (12.75mm) needles, or size needed to obtain gauge.

GAUGE

5.75 sts and 7 rows = 4" (10cm) over Drop Stitch patt.

FINISHED MEASUREMENTS

28" (71cm) wide x 14" (46cm) long

FINISHING MATERIALS

1 shell shawl pin (Dritz)
38 blue, yellow, and orange beads

YARN HARMONY PAIRING PAGE 64

SCHEMATICS PAGE 101

FALL PAIRINGS

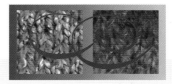

The fall pairings blend deep, rich yarn colors. These rich seasonal colors include ochre and golden yellows, rust and dark oranges, maroon and brick reds, plum and amethyst purples, sapphire and royal blues, and olive and forest greens. The fall medium to bulky weight yarns include cotton, bamboo, silk, mohair, and wool yarns in ribbon, bouclé, chenille, slubbed, and multi-strand textures. ✲ The Fall Purse and Wrap patterns each represent two pairings in this section. The Fall Purse *(page 82)* is knit with analogous orange rust wool and slubbed yarns *(page 72)* for a durable texture. Complementary purple wool and bouclé yarn colors *(page 76)* are paired in the warm and stylish Fall Wrap *(page 83)*. The seasonal swatches reflect the multicolored shades and tones of the ever-changing splendor of the fall.

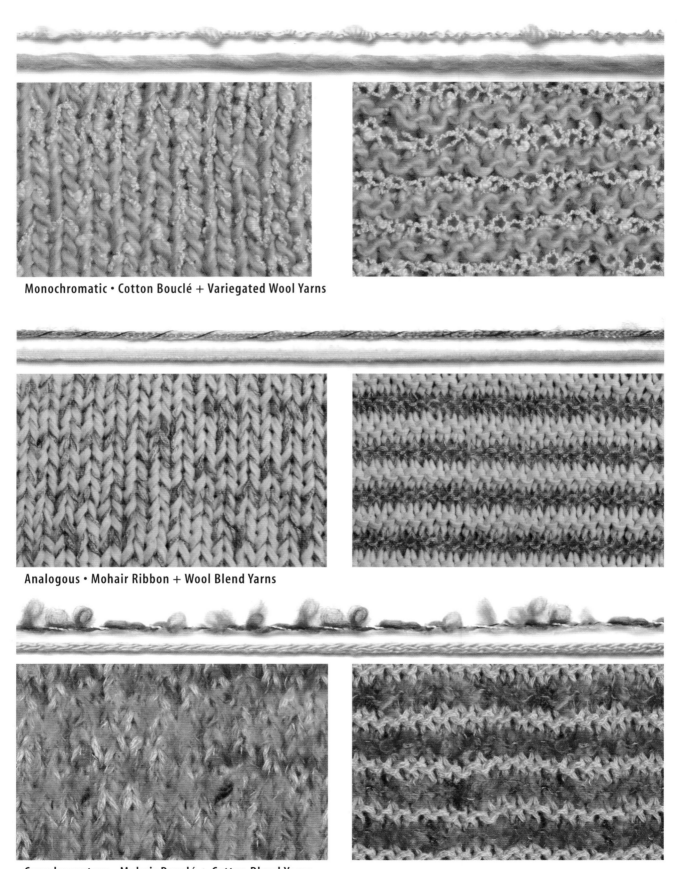

Monochromatic • Cotton Bouclé + Variegated Wool Yarns

Analogous • Mohair Ribbon + Wool Blend Yarns

Complementary • Mohair Bouclé + Cotton Blend Yarns

Black + Color • Bamboo + Cotton Yarns

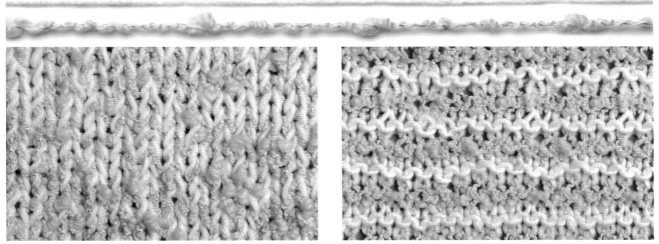

White + Color • Wool Blend + Cotton Bouclé Blend Yarns

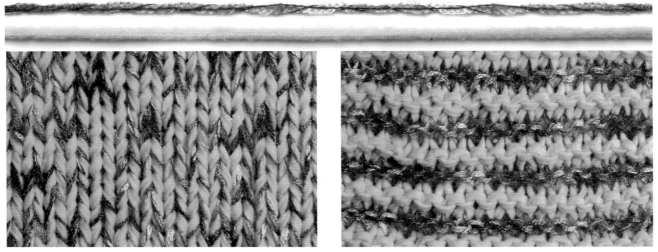

Neutral + Color • Mohair Ribbon + Wool Blend Yarns

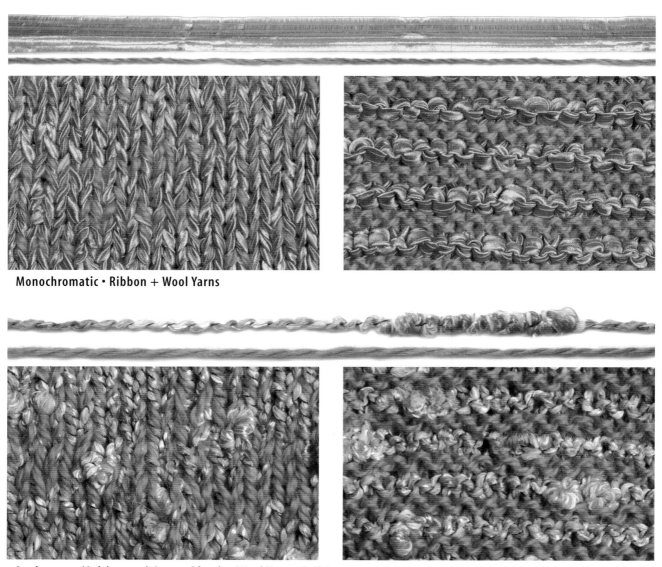

Monochromatic • Ribbon + Wool Yarns

Analogous • Multi-strand Cotton Blend + Wool Yarns, *Fall Purse Pattern page 82*

Complementary • Mohair Ribbon + Mohair Ribbon Yarns

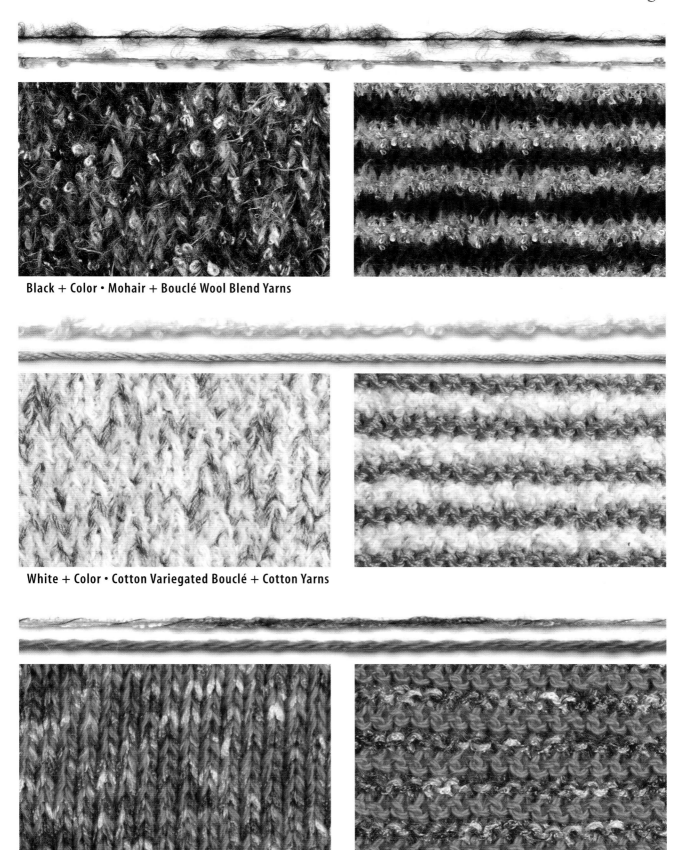

Black + Color • Mohair + Bouclé Wool Blend Yarns

White + Color • Cotton Variegated Bouclé + Cotton Yarns

Neutral + Color • Mohair Ribbon + Wool Yarns

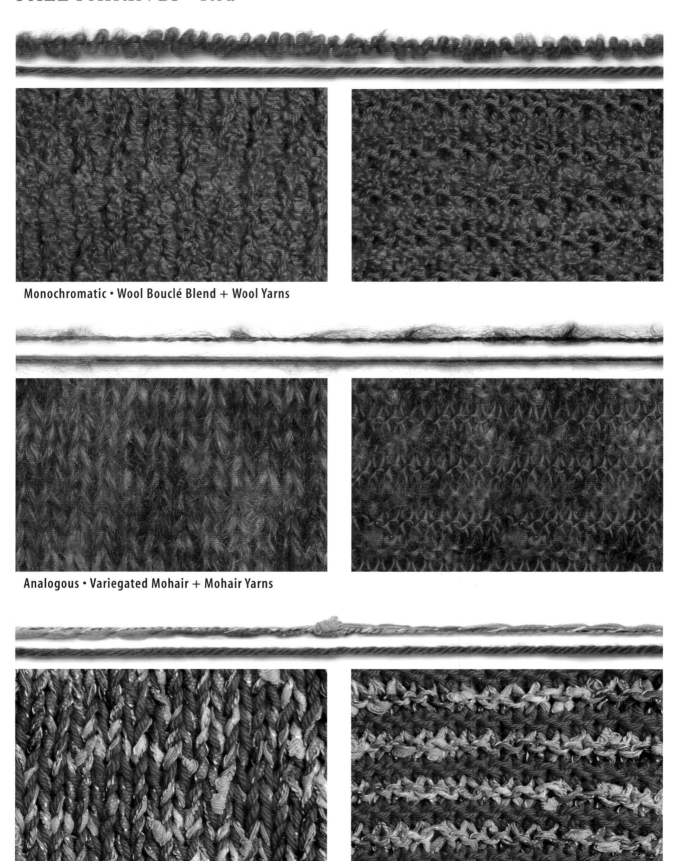

Monochromatic • Wool Bouclé Blend + Wool Yarns

Analogous • Variegated Mohair + Mohair Yarns

Complementary • Multi-strand Cotton Blend + Wool Blend Yarns

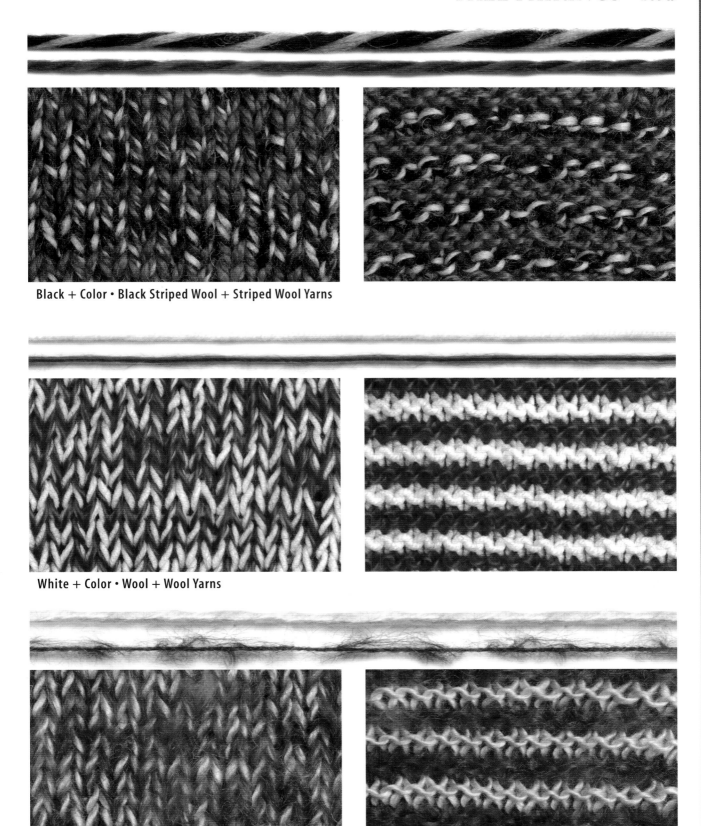

Black + Color • Black Striped Wool + Striped Wool Yarns

White + Color • Wool + Wool Yarns

Neutral + Color • Silk Blend + Variegated Mohair Yarns

Monochromatic • Wool Blend + Silk Blend Yarns

Analogous • Wool Slub + Wool Yarns

Complementary • Bouclé Wool Blend + Cotton Yarns, *Fall Wrap Pattern page 83*

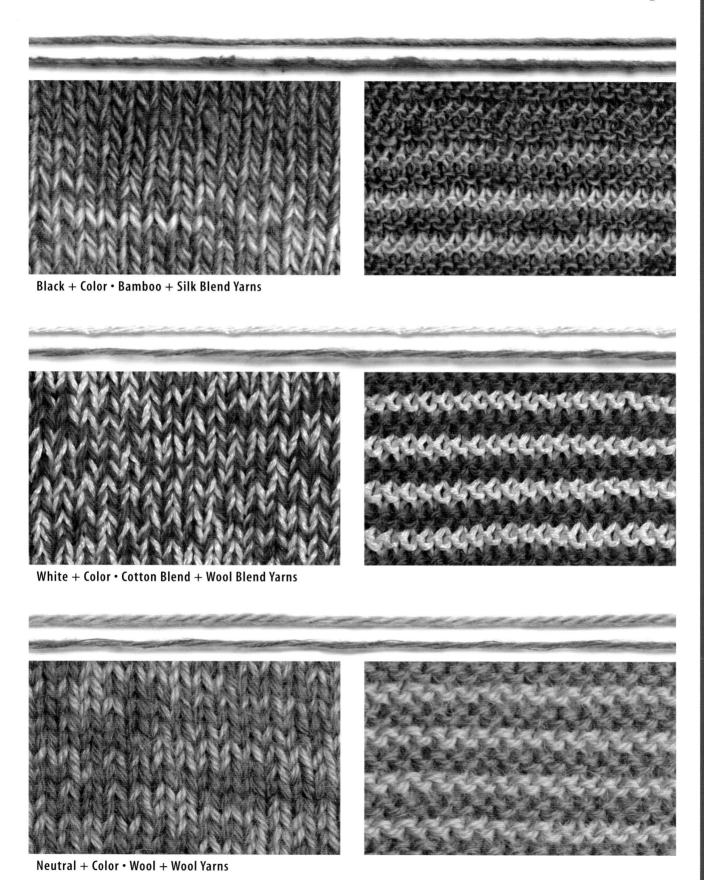

Black + Color • Bamboo + Silk Blend Yarns

White + Color • Cotton Blend + Wool Blend Yarns

Neutral + Color • Wool + Wool Yarns

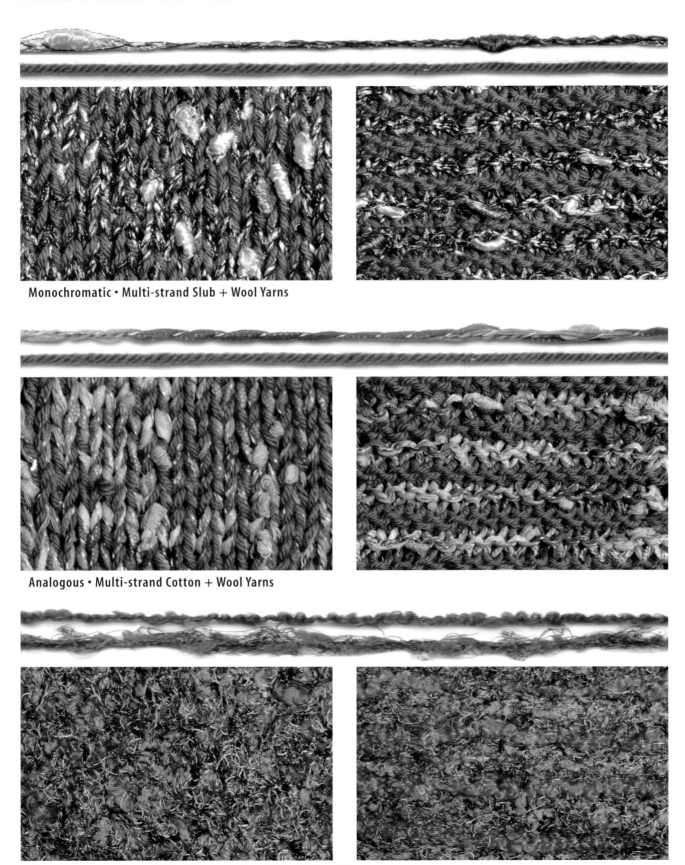

Monochromatic • Multi-strand Slub + Wool Yarns

Analogous • Multi-strand Cotton + Wool Yarns

Complementary • Bouclé Wool Blend + Bouclé Wool Blend Yarns

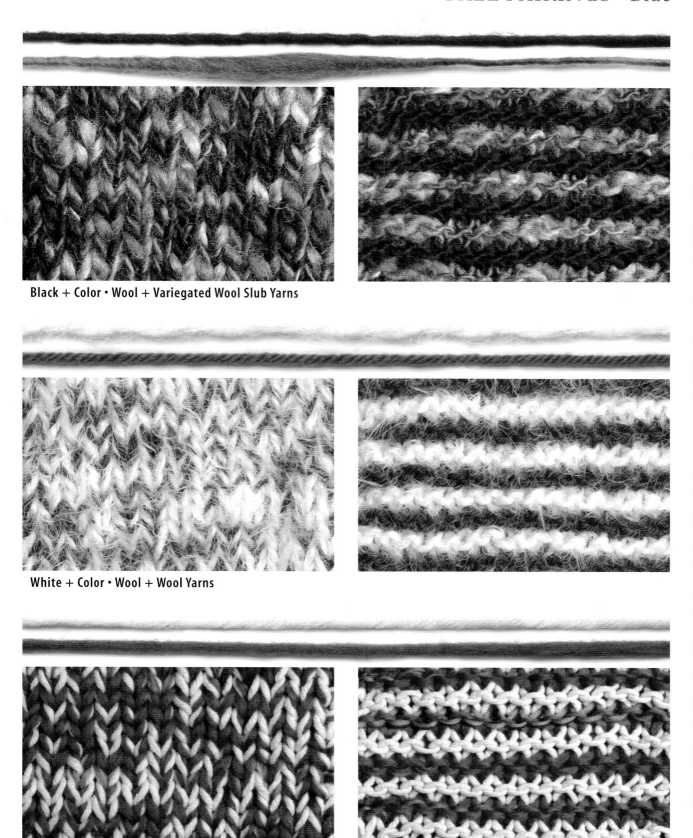

Black + Color • Wool + Variegated Wool Slub Yarns

White + Color • Wool + Wool Yarns

Neutral + Color • Cotton Blend + Wool Blend Yarns

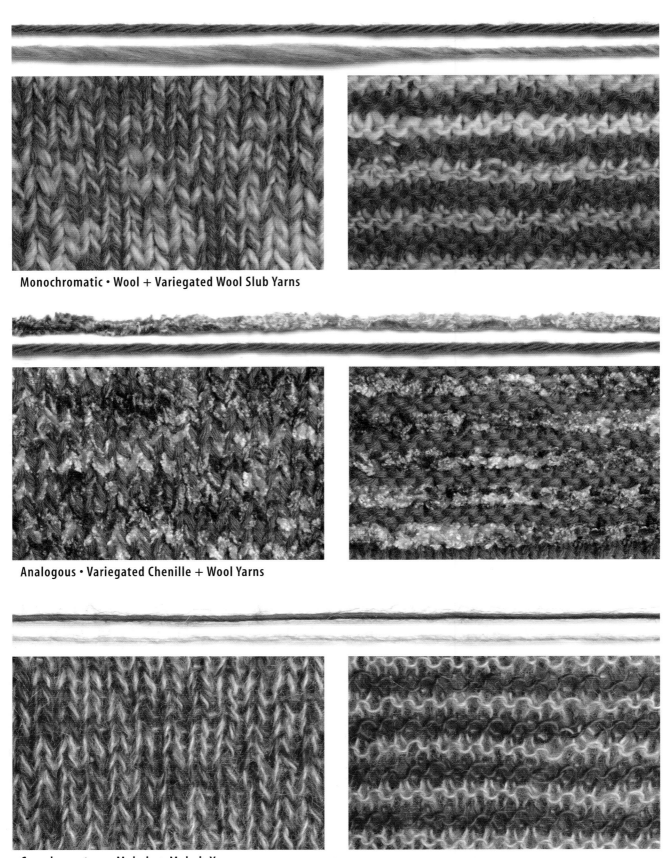

Monochromatic • Wool + Variegated Wool Slub Yarns

Analogous • Variegated Chenille + Wool Yarns

Complementary • Mohair + Mohair Yarns

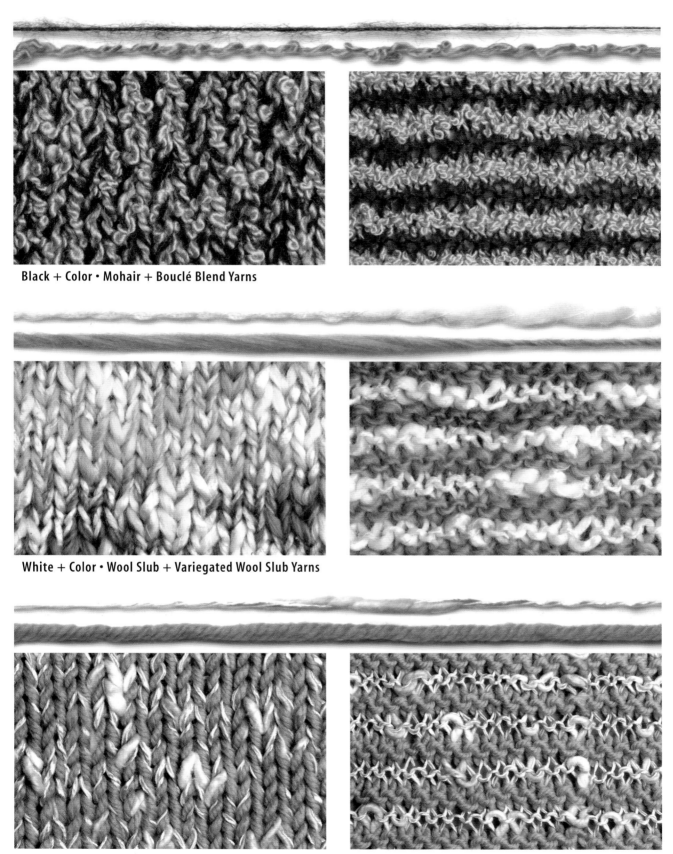

Black + Color • Mohair + Bouclé Blend Yarns

White + Color • Wool Slub + Variegated Wool Slub Yarns

Neutral + Color • Variegated Cotton Blend Slub + Wool Yarns

FALL PURSE

This practical yet stylish all-purpose purse uses analogous colors to brighten the orange hues of the blended bouclé and wool yarns. You'll adore the glossy black licorice Jelly Yarn trim for the resilient weatherproof bottom. The combination of soft wool and shiny vinyl make this uniquely designed Fall Purse a sassy fashion accessory.

FRONT AND BACK (ONE PIECE)

With US 7 needles, CO 45 sts with 1 strand of A and 1 strand of B held tog.

Work in St st until piece measures 18" (45.75cm).

BO loosely.

TOP EDGING

Fold the front and back piece in half. With 1 strand of B, sew the sides tog. Leave the top of the bag open. With 2 strands of C held tog and US 8 circular needle, pick up 90 sts around the top of the bag. Place a marker and begin working in rounds.

Rnd 1: P around.

Rnd 2: K around.

BO loosely, purlwise.

BOTTOM

With US 8 needles and 2 strands of C held tog, CO 25 sts.

Rows 1–6: Slip 1st st purlwise. K across.

Rows 7–12: K2tog, K to last 2 sts, K2tog. (13 sts)

Rows 13–77: Slip 1st st purlwise. K across.

Rows 78–83: K into front and back of next st to Make 1, K across to last 2 sts, Make 1, K1. (25 sts)

Rows 84–89: Slip 1st st purlwise. K across.

BO loosely.

HANDLES (MAKE 2)

With size 8 double-pointed needles and 2 strands of C held tog, CO 3 sts.

Work I-cord 21" (53.25cm) long.

BO.

FINISHING AND ASSEMBLY

BOTTOM

Form the piece by folding the end up, aligning the sides with the bottom to create the finished shape. Pin in place and sew with 1 strand of C. Repeat for all 4 corners. Pin the WS of the bottom to the RS of the bag, making sure the bag fits inside the bottom corners. Sew the bottom to the bag with black thread and sewing needle.

HANDLES

Attach the handles 2" (5cm) from the side of the bag and 1" (2.5cm) down from 1st row of C. Sew the buttons on at each end. Repeat for both sides.

PURSE FASTENER

Attach the fastener to the inside top of the bag at the center.

Carrie A. Sullivan

EASY

YARN

A: 3 balls Berroco *Monet* 49yds (44m) / 50g (42% rayon, 36% acrylic, 13% cotton, 9% nylon) Color: 3366
B: 2 balls Debbie Bliss *Alpaca Silk* DK 71yds (65m) / 50g (80% baby alpaca, 20% silk) Color: 10
C: 2 balls Jelly Yarn *Fine* 85yds (78m) / 200g (100% vinyl) Color: Black Licorice

NEEDLES

US 7 (4.5mm) and US 8 (5mm) straight needles, US 8 (5mm) 24" (61cm) circular needles and US 8 (5mm) double-pointed needles, or size needed to obtain gauge.

GAUGE

16 sts and 24 rows = 4" (10cm) with 1 strand of A and 1 strand of B held together over Stockinette stitch patt using size US 7 needles.
16 sts and 24 rows = 4" (10cm) with 2 strands of C held tog over Garter stitch patt using size US 8 needles.

FINISHED MEASUREMENTS

11" (28cm) wide x 9.5" (24.25cm) high

FINISHING MATERIALS

4 - 1" (2.5cm) gold buttons
Purse fastener

YARN HARMONY PAIRING PAGE 72

SCHEMATICS PAGE 101

FALL WRAP

Is it a shrug or a wrap with sleeves? Surround yourself in this velvety soft Fall Wrap. Complementary variegated bouclé and solid wool-blend purple yarns are used in this simple beginner's project. Solid-wool Aran yarn is knit for the top and bottom edges and all-in-one sleeve cuffs. For evening wear, the vibrant colors work best with black.

WRAP

Note: When changing colors, twist yarn on WS to prevent holes in the work.

With A, CO 144 sts.

Row 1: K6, (YO, K1) 22x, K2tog 44x, (K1, YO) 22x, end K6.

Row 2: P across.

Row 3: K6, join B, (YO, K1) 22x, K2tog 44x, (K1, YO) 22x, join another ball of A and end K6.

Row 4: With A, P6, with B, P across to last 6 sts, with A, P6.

Row 5: With A, K6, with B, (YO, K1) 22x, K2tog 44x, (K1, YO) 22x, with A, end K6.

Row 6: Repeat Row 4.

Row 7: With A, K6, with B, K across to last 6 sts, with A, K6.

Row 8: With A, P6, with B, P across to last 6 sts, with A, P6.

Repeat rows 7 and 8 until the wrap measures 13 1/2" (34.25cm) from beginning, ending on a K row.

Next Row: Drop B, with A, P across.

Next Row: K across.

BO loosely.

FINISHING

Fold the wrap in half lengthwise and sew 3" (7.5cm) seams at both ends to form the cuffs. Sew the shell buttons on each cuff.

Kathleen Greco

EASY

YARN

A: 1 ball Louisa Harding *Kashmir Aran* 99yds (90m) / 50g (55% merino wool, 35% microfiber, 10% cashmere) Color: 16

B: 3 balls Louisa Harding *Liberty Bouclé* 83yds (75m) / 50g (60% mohair, 25% viscose, 15% polyamide) Color: 07

NEEDLES

US 13 (9mm) needles, or size needed to obtain gauge.

GAUGE

9 sts and 13 rows = 4" (10cm) over Stockinette stitch patt with B.

FINISHED MEASUREMENTS

48" (122cm) wide x 14" (35.5m) long

FINISHING MATERIALS

2 shell buttons

YARN HARMONY PAIRING PAGE 76

SCHEMATICS PAGE 101

WINTER PAIRINGS

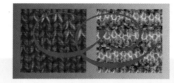

The winter pairings display a wonderful collection of deep yarn colors. These lush seasonal colors include goldenrod and dark yellows, auburn and dark rust oranges, burgundy and dark ruby reds, wine and indigo purples, navy and cobalt blues, and emerald and dark greens. The medium to bulky weight swatches include cotton, silk, mohair, and wool yarns in bouclé, slubbed, chenille, and multi-strand textures. ✳ The Winter Scarf and Sweater patterns each represent two pairings in this section. The Winter Scarf *(page 99)* is knit with white and blue variegated wool and mohair yarns *(page 95)*. Monochromatic burgundy red silk and wool yarn colors *(page 90)* are combined in the stylish Winter Sweater *(page 98)*. Winter swatches blend deep colors with the cuddly and warm knitwear of the season.

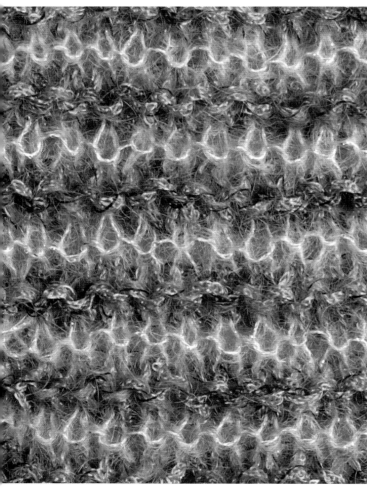

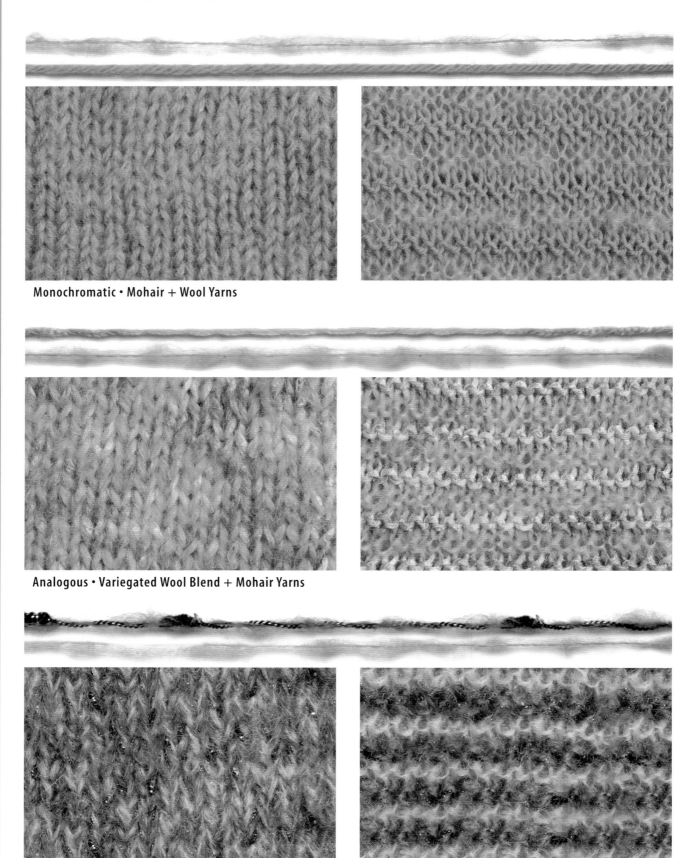

Monochromatic • Mohair + Wool Yarns

Analogous • Variegated Wool Blend + Mohair Yarns

Complementary • Multi-strand Wool Blend + Mohair Yarns

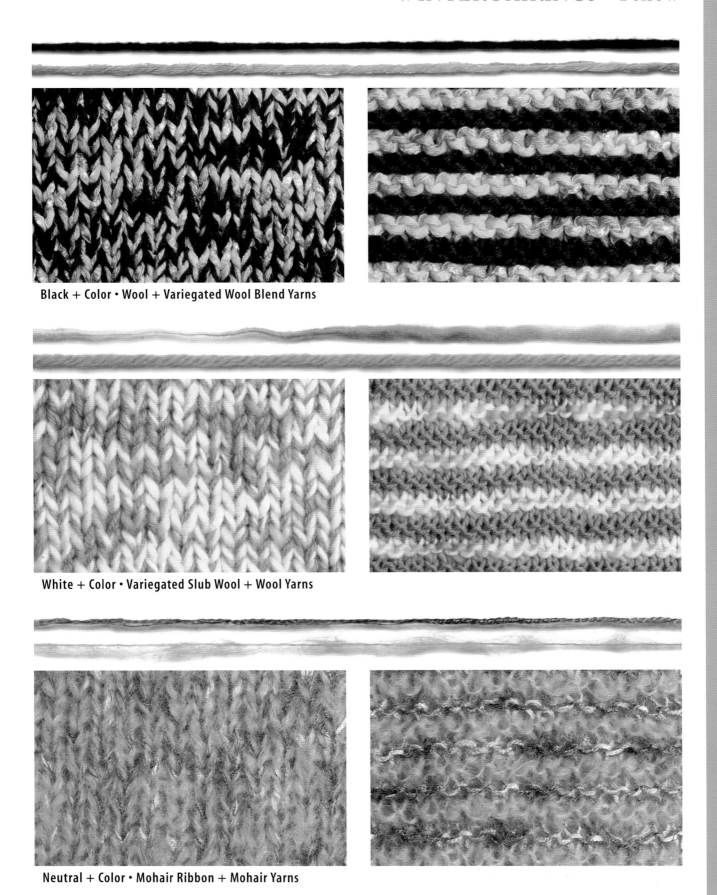

Black + Color • Wool + Variegated Wool Blend Yarns

White + Color • Variegated Slub Wool + Wool Yarns

Neutral + Color • Mohair Ribbon + Mohair Yarns

Monochromatic • Wool + Wool Blend Yarns

Analogous • Variegated Mohair + Wool Blend Yarns

Complementary • Variegated Wool + Wool Yarns

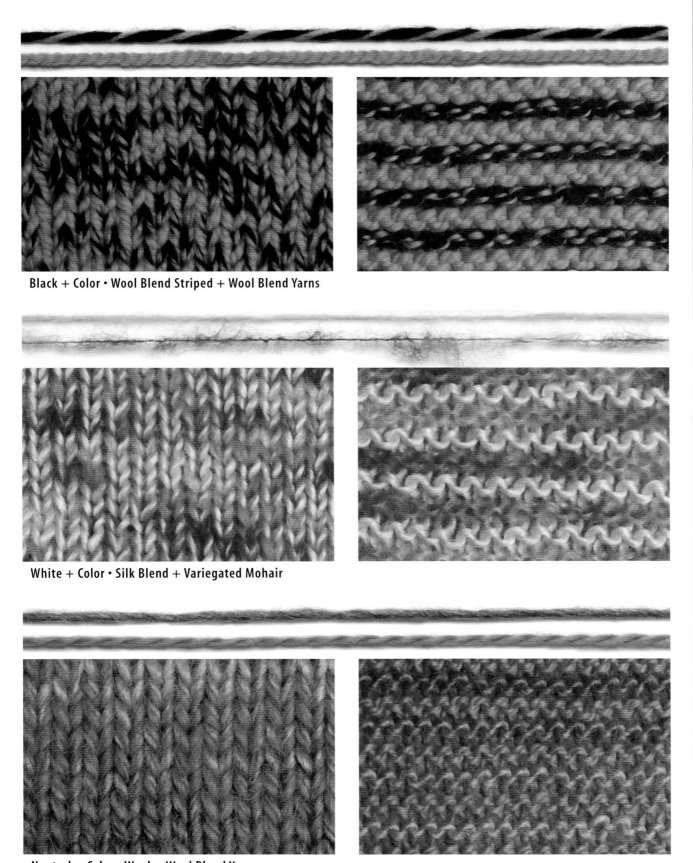

Black + Color • Wool Blend Striped + Wool Blend Yarns

White + Color • Silk Blend + Variegated Mohair

Neutral + Color • Wool + Wool Blend Yarns

Monochromatic • Silk Blend + Wool Yarns, *Winter Sweater Pattern page 98*

Analogous • Wool + Wool Yarns

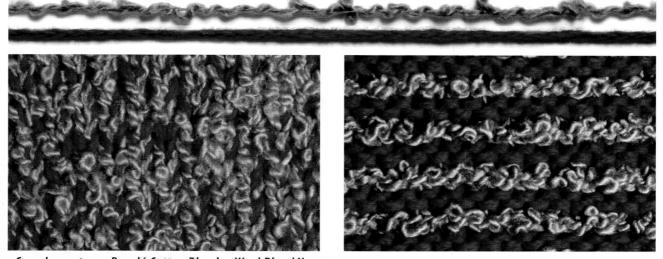

Complementary • Bouclé Cotton Blend + Wool Blend Yarns

Black + Color • Wool Blend + Chenille Yarns

White + Color • Bouclé Wool Blend + Wool Yarns

Neutral + Color • Mohair Ribbon + Silk Blend Yarns

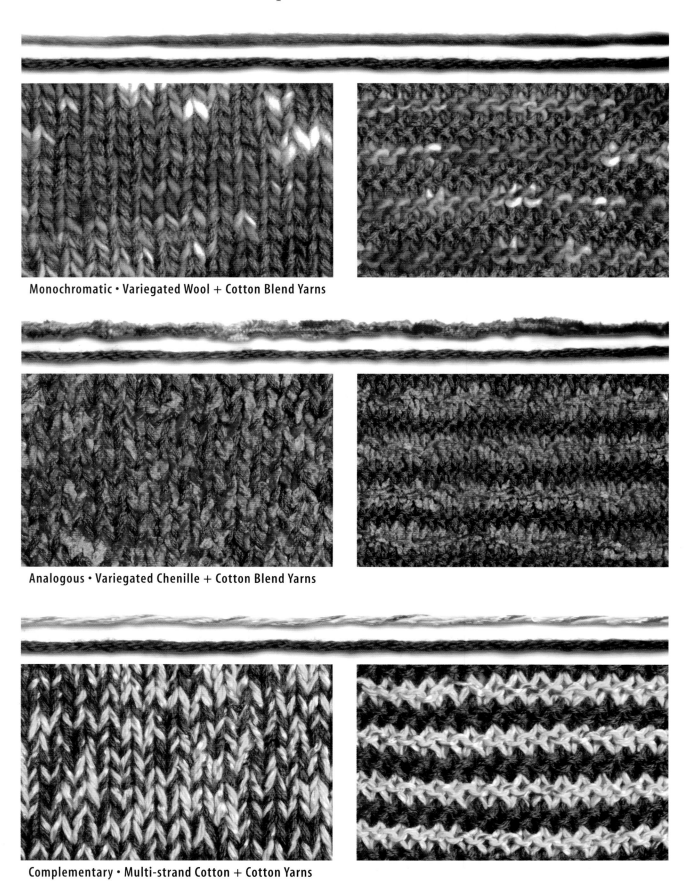

Monochromatic • Variegated Wool + Cotton Blend Yarns

Analogous • Variegated Chenille + Cotton Blend Yarns

Complementary • Multi-strand Cotton + Cotton Yarns

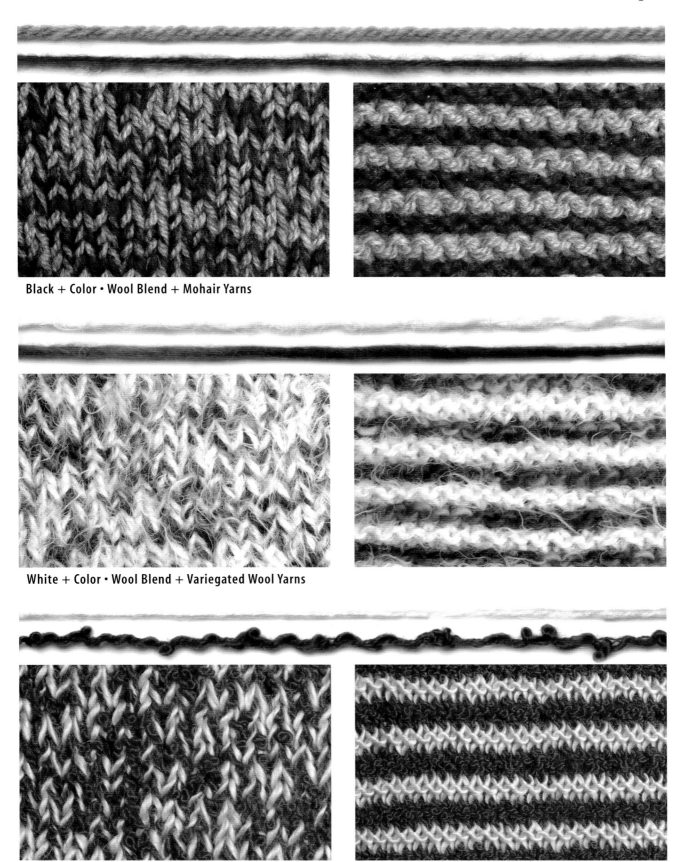

Black + Color • Wool Blend + Mohair Yarns

White + Color • Wool Blend + Variegated Wool Yarns

Neutral + Color • Silk Blend + Bouclé Wool Blend Yarns

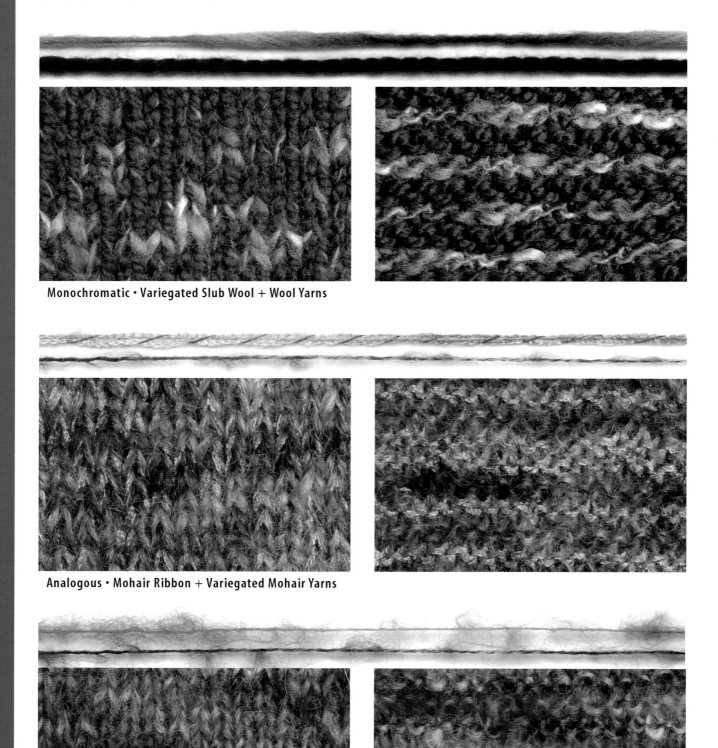

Monochromatic • Variegated Slub Wool + Wool Yarns

Analogous • Mohair Ribbon + Variegated Mohair Yarns

Complementary • Variegated Mohair + Variegated Mohair Yarns

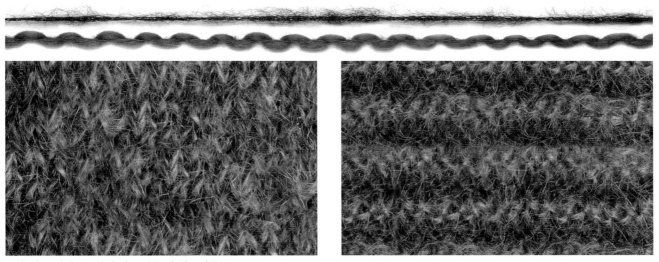

Black + Color • Mohair + Wool Blend Yarns

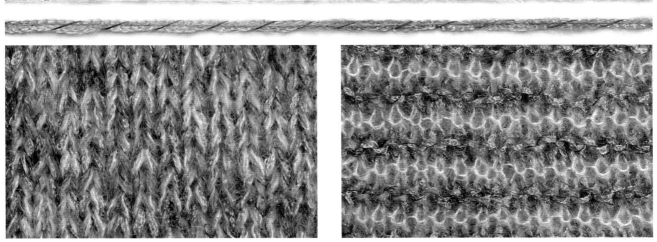

White + Color • Mohair + Mohair Ribbon Yarns, *Winter Scarf Pattern page 99*

Neutral + Color • Wool + Wool Yarns

Monochromatic • Cotton Blend + Wool Yarns

Analogous • Variegated Mohair + Cotton Blend Yarns

Complementary • Silk + Mohair Yarns

Black + Color • Bouclé Wool Blend + Wool Blend Yarns

White + Color • Variegated Slub Wool Blend + Wool Yarns

Neutral + Color • Wool + Variegated Wool Yarns

WINTER SWEATER

This Winter Sweater features a blend of monochromatic colors and a feminine V-neck design. Soft alpaca wool was used to knit the bodice and long bell-shaped cuffs. The top, shoulders, and upper sleeves are knit with a soft silk variegated yarn. The deep burgundy color brings a taste of winter to the luxurious yarns of the season. Side slits on the bottom edge and cuffs make this cozy sweater a perfect fit.

2 x 1 RIBBING STITCH PATTERN
Row 1: *K2, P1, repeat from * to end.

Row 2: *K1, P2, repeat from * to end.

Repeat Rows 1 and 2.

FRONT
With A and larger needles, CO 84 (90, 96, 99) sts.

Row 1: (WS) P across.

Row 2: Work in 2 x 1 Ribbing for 10 (10.5, 11, 11.5)" / 25.5 (26.75, 28, 29.25) cm, ending on a WS row. Change to B and smaller needles, and K increasing 8 (10, 10, 9) sts evenly across row. (92, 100, 106, 108 sts)

Work in St st for 5 (5.5, 6, 7)" / 12.75 (14, 15.25, 17.75) cm, ending on a RS row.

ARMHOLE AND V-NECK
BO 3 sts at the beginning of the next 3 rows. (83, 91, 97, 99 sts)

Next Row: BO 3 sts, K across 40 (44, 47, 48) sts, join a 2nd ball of yarn and K to end.

Next Row: Working both sides of the V-neck at the same time, P across.

Next Row: K to last 3 sts of left front, K2tog, K1, K1 (with second ball of yarn), SKP, K to end of right front.

Continue working in St st, decreasing 1 st at each side of V-neck every RS row, until armhole measures 7.5 (8, 8.5, 9)" / 19 (20, 21.5, 23) cm. BO loosely.

BACK
Work as for front through first row of B.

Work in St st for 5 (5.5, 6, 7)" / 12.75 (14, 15.25, 17.75) cm, ending on a RS row.

ARMHOLE
BO 3 sts at the beginning of the next 4 rows. (80, 88, 94, 96 sts)

Work even in St st until armhole measures 7.5 (8, 8.5, 9)" / 19 (20, 21.5, 23) cm.

BO loosely.

SLEEVES (MAKE 2)
With A and larger needles, CO 60 (60, 60, 63) sts.

Row 1: (WS) P across.

Rows 2 and 4: K2tog 3x, work in 2 x 1 Ribbing to last 6 sts, K2tog 3x. (48, 48, 48, 51 sts)

INTERMEDIATE

YARN
A: 5, 5, 5, 6 balls Plymouth Yarn *Baby Alpaca Grande* 110yds (100m) / 100g (100% baby alpaca) Color: 2020
B: 5, 6, 6, 7 balls Alchemy *Synchronicity* 110yds (100m) / 50g (50% silk, 50% wool) Color: 25c

NEEDLES
US 10 (6mm) and US 8 (5mm) needles, or size needed to obtain gauge.

GAUGE
20 sts and 19 rows = 4" (10cm) over 2 x 1 Ribbing stitch patt with A using US 10 needles.
22 sts and 27 rows = 4" (10cm) over Stockinette stitch patt with B using US 8 needles.

FINISHED MEASUREMENTS
34 (36, 38, 40)" / 86.25 (91.5, 96.5, 101.5) cm wide x 22.5 (24, 25.5, 27.5)" / 57 (61, 64.75, 69.75) cm long

YARN HARMONY PAIRING page 90

SCHEMATICS page 102

pattern continued on page 102

Winter Scarf

You'll love the unique design of this soft, tubular scarf, knit in the round on circular needles. Blue variegated and white mohair and silk yarns are used to create the stripes. The big ruffle ends serve to accentuate this funky, warm accessory, while the extra-long length promises plenty of scarf to go around.

SCARF

With 2 strands of A, CO 240 sts. Straighten sts on needle. Place marker and join.

Rnd 1: K around.

Rnd 2: P around.

Rnd 3: Drop A and join 1 strand of B and K around.

Rnd 4: K around.

Rnd 5: K2tog around. (120 sts)

RUFFLE

Rnds 6–18: K every rnd.

Rnd 19: K2tog around. (60 sts)

Rnd 20: *K1, K2tog* repeat from * to * around. (40 sts)

STRIPES

Rnds 21–31: K every rnd.

Rnds 32–35: Drop B, join 2 strands of A, K every rnd.

Rnds 36–46: Drop A, join B, K every rnd.

Rnds 47–50: Drop B, join 2 strands of A, K every rnd.

Rnds 51–61: Drop A, join B, K every rnd.

Rnds 62–65: Drop B, join 2 strands of A, K every rnd.

BODY

Drop A, join B, K every rnd for 53" (134.75cm) or desired length.

STRIPES

Repeat Rnds 32–65.

Next 11 Rnds: Drop A, join B, K every rnd.

RUFFLE

Next Rnd: *K1, Inc 1 st in next st* repeat from * to * around. (60 sts)

Next Rnd: (Inc 1 st in next st) around. (120 sts)

Next 13 Rnds: K around.

Next Rnd: (Inc 1 st in next st) around. (240 sts)

Next Rnd: K around.

Next Rnd: Drop B and join 2 strands of A and K around.

Next Rnd: P around.

BO purlwise loosely.

FINISHING

On one end of the scarf, weave B above the ruffle with the yarn needle. Gather the stitches and secure with a knot. Repeat for the other end.

Kathleen Greco

EASY

YARN

A: 1 ball Rowan *Kidsilk Haze* 229yds (210m) / 25g (70% super kid mohair, 30% silk) Color: 580 Grace

B: 2 balls Louisa Harding Yarns *Impression* 154yds (141m) / 50g (84% polyamide, 16% mohair) Color: 10 Lagoon

NEEDLES

US 7 (4.5mm) circular 12" (30.5cm) needles, or size needed to obtain gauge.

FINISHED MEASUREMENTS

3.5" (9cm) wide x 78" (2m) long

FINISHING MATERIALS

Yarn needle

YARN HARMONY PAIRING PAGE 94

SCHEMATICS PAGE 102

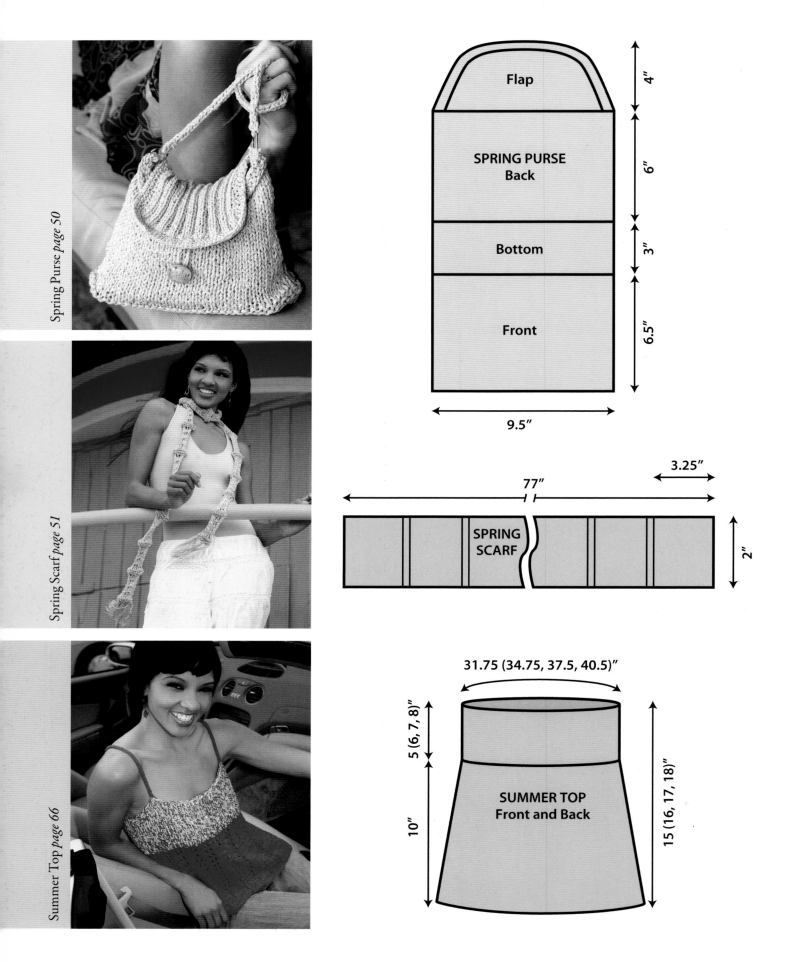

Spring Purse *page 50*

Spring Scarf *page 51*

Summer Top *page 66*

Flap

SPRING PURSE
Back

Bottom

Front

4"

6"

3"

6.5"

9.5"

3.25"

77"

SPRING
SCARF

2"

31.75 (34.75, 37.5, 40.5)"

5 (6, 7, 8)"

10"

SUMMER TOP
Front and Back

15 (16, 17, 18)"

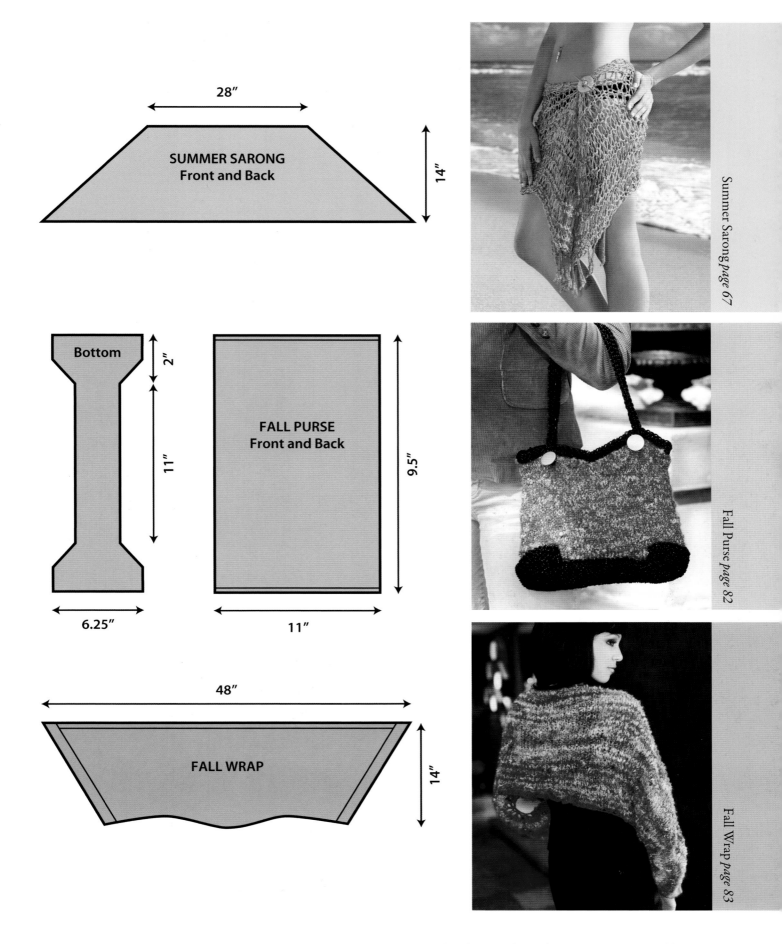

28"

SUMMER SARONG
Front and Back

14"

Bottom

2"

11"

FALL PURSE
Front and Back

9.5"

6.25"

11"

48"

FALL WRAP

14"

Summer Sarong page 67

Fall Purse page 82

Fall Wrap page 83

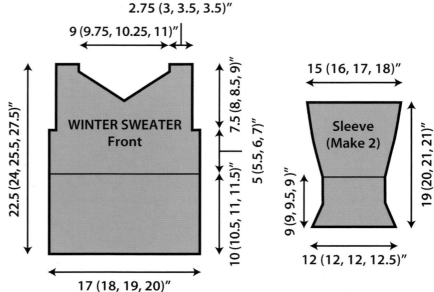

2.75 (3, 3.5, 3.5)"

9 (9.75, 10.25, 11)"

**WINTER SWEATER
Front**

22.5 (24, 25.5, 27.5)"

7.5 (8, 8.5, 9)"

5 (5.5, 6, 7)"

10 (10.5, 11, 11.5)"

17 (18, 19, 20)"

15 (16, 17, 18)"

Sleeve
(Make 2)

19 (20, 21, 21)"

9 (9, 9.5, 9)"

12 (12, 12, 12.5)"

pattern continued from page 98

Rows 3 and 5: P3, work in 2 x 1 Ribbing to last 3 sts, P3.

Work in 2 x 1 Ribbing until sleeve measures 9 (9, 9.5, 9)" / 22.75 (22.75, 24, 22.75) cm, ending on a WS row.

Change to B and smaller needles, and K increasing 1 st at each end of row. (50, 50, 50, 53 sts)

Work in St st, increasing 1 st each end of row every 8th row 2x, then every 4th row 10x (13x, 15x, 16x). (74, 80, 84, 89 sts)

Work even until sleeve measures 19 (20, 21, 21)" / 48 (50.75, 53.25, 53.25) cm.

BO loosely.

FINISHING

Sew the shoulder seams. Join the sleeves to the front and back. Sew the underarm seams, leaving a 3" (7.5cm) slit at the cuff. Then, sew the side seams leaving a 3" (7.5cm) slit at the bottom.

Kathleen Greco

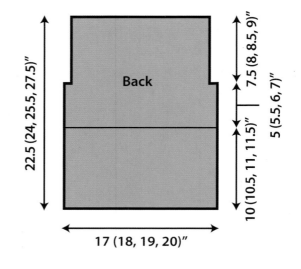

Back

22.5 (24, 25.5, 27.5)"

7.5 (8, 8.5, 9)"

5 (5.5, 6, 7)"

10 (10.5, 11, 11.5)"

17 (18, 19, 20)"

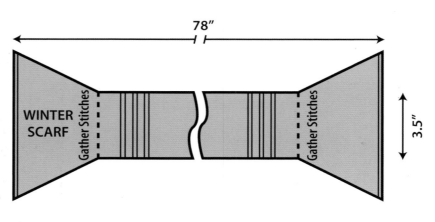

78"

**WINTER
SCARF**

Gather Stitches

Gather Stitches

3.5"